KARATE BREAKING TECHNIQUES

KARATE

Photographs by Marco A. Vega · Sketches by Nicholas Weih

Rutland · Vermont : Tokyo · Japan

BREAKING
TECHNIQUES

with Practical Applications for Self-Defense

by JACK HIBBARD

CHARLES E. TUTTLE COMPANY

Published by the Charles E. Tuttle Company, Inc.
of Rutland, Vermont & Tokyo, Japan
with editorial offices at
2-6 Suido 1-chome, Bunkyo-ku, Tokyo 112

© 1981 by Charles E. Tuttle Publishing Co., Inc.

LCC Card No. 80-50893
ISBN 0-8048-1876-2

First printing, 1981
First paperback edition, 1993
Second printing, 1993

PRINTED IN JAPAN

To Linda, my wife
who fills the past, present, and future
of my Aura with happiness

■ ■ Table of Contents

■ ■ Introduction

It has long been my impression that there was a genuine
need for a book on breaking techniques. Thousands of
students search for guidance in this field, only to be turned
away by the lack of knowledge and enthusiasm in their
instructors. Yet, the desire persists. Groping for instruction
and leadership, they flounder on year by year making the
rounds of different schools. But the pattern rarely changes.
Locked in their training, instructors rely on stereotyped
breaking techniques. Few are lucky enough to find a school
with the innovative spark necessary to rejuvenate enthusiasm in the art of breaking. Most forfeit the search and
resign themselves to train in other areas. It is an unfortunate
waste of talent.

I hope that this book will fill the void. It is not my inten-
tion to glamorize my subject, but rather, to place this art in
its proper perspective. The ease of some techniques is
clearly shown, as well as the difficulty of other breaks which
are defined so as not to confuse the novice. I have made
this an in-depth study of breaking techniques, in coordination with their application as effective self-defense moves.
The ultimate purpose of breaking is self-defense. To acquire
the ability to break without regard for its proper function
in self-defense is not in the true spirit of the art.

Breaking is not an easy field of endeavor; its pursuit is
often discouraging. Years of staunch dedication are necessary to excel, for to break effectively requires concentration

of mind, the ability to properly utilize generated power, and the perseverance to develop speed. The book includes sections that develop these areas one by one. Each section is complemented by exercises and techniques necessary for a well-rounded program. Following this regimen will guide you in your breaking career, thereby improving your physical capabilities as well as your mental attitude. It is my hope that all who read this will come away with new insight and knowledge in a fascinating area of karate.

I wish to express my sincere appreciation to Mr. Arthur Cohen, whose generosity to his students is exceeded only by his dedication toward the advancement of the martial arts. I also wish to thank Anthony Buscaino, John Dunn, Joe Scarione, and my brother Pete who assisted as models. A special thanks is in order for Joe Alessi, Jimmy Chin, Dave Davis, and Steve Ganim, who unselfishly devoted endless time and energy to ensure that each technique was more impressive than the last. The section on women's breaking was demonstrated by my sister Peggy, whose ability is surpassed only by her beauty.

To Marco A. Vega, for his excellent photographic work, and Margaret Sauers Vega, his lovely assistant, I am indebted for the arduous task they undertook and completed with planned professionalism. The illustrations were drawn by the expert hand of Nicholas Weih.

PART 1

Preparation for Breaking

The breaks demonstrated in this book, if properly executed, should cause no harm to any person who is physically sound and in good health. However, because of the injury factor involved, breaking should be performed only with proper supervision or by experienced practitioners of the art. The author and publisher can accept no responsibility for accident or injury sustained during the execution of any break presented in this book.

■ Why Breaking Is Important

Each movement in karate, from the time a student first learns it to the time he has perfected it, will require thousands of repetitions. However, the repetitions will be irrelevant if the student is not actually striking an object and feeling the impact of the blows. Without this experience, he will have no idea of how great his power is and how he can control it. Breaking is a way of applying power in a controlled method designed to measure the force of the blow.

Making contact with a solid object has a beneficial effect, psychologically as well as physiologically. It conditions the mind to control what the body is doing and to measure the amount of pain it can tolerate. The capacity to accept pain from the shock of a blow on impact is a mental attitude derived from repeated contact with a surface that offers resistance.

An instructor can evaluate the accuracy of a beginner's blows, when directed into the air, because the speed of delivery is within the range that the eye can see. However, with advanced students, the speed of delivery increases, and evaluation becomes more difficult. Breaking, therefore, acts as a visual aid to the instructor, for accuracy can be monitored and progress ascertained.

The beginner continually hears of the devastating potential of a karate movement. However, unless his training includes making contact with a solid object, he will fail to realize what effect these movements may have on himself or an opponent. Once the student becomes aware of each aspect of his movement, he will advance rapidly in the art.

■ Focus

The word *focus* is probably one of the most often heard yet least understood words in the martial arts' vocabulary. Focus is the ability to control the muscles of the body in a coordinated effort and then contract them to their maximum degree upon impact. The full development of this ability is what distinguishes a respectable student from one whose interest lies solely in acquiring rank instead of knowledge. Unfortunately, many contemporary students have only a vague or distorted understanding of this essential phase of training.

In order to gain maximum efficiency in a movement, you need a general knowledge of the human anatomy. A certain series of principles must be followed for focus to materialize. For each technique requiring focus, you bring different muscles into play; contract some and relax others at the precise moment of impact. Precision timing is essential if you want results.

There are approximately 600 muscles in the human body. As a muscle is contracted (tensed), energy is produced. This energy is released as pressure through a predetermined point on the body. The number of muscles contracted, and their degree of tension, is in direct proportion to the amount of pressure (focus) that will be exerted upon impact. Developing this ability requires endless hours of muscle contraction and relaxation while working on techniques. No movement in karate should ever be executed without contracting every muscle possible. When a technique is practiced, it should be done slowly, with concentration centered on tensing the entire muscular group involved in that particular movement. The deeper the concentration, the tenser the contraction of the muscle; and the tenser the contraction, the stronger the muscle grows.

Another phase of development derived from this method of training is the ability to increase the number of muscles that can be controlled during a technique. The more muscles controlled at the moment of impact, the greater the amount of pressure at that point. Speed is important, but no matter how swiftly you move, the force from speed alone is relatively small. It is only when you put the entire muscular power of the body behind the movement that you can apply maximum force at the point of contact.

Synchronization of speed and muscular contraction is the finale to a specific program of body movements. First the hips and stomach muscles, the slow strong group, must start their move toward the target before the faster, but weaker, group in the arms and legs. They must be coordinated while in motion to reach both maximum strength and momentum. As the arm or leg nears its objective, it reaches maximum speed. At the moment of impact, the entire muscular system is tensed. Thus, you have transformed speed into power and released the energy created within the body as focus. This energy is released instantaneously at the moment of contact with the target.

■ Conditioning the Hands

The need for conditioning the hands becomes evident as soon as you feel the pain of the first breaking exercise you attempt. To understand the need for conditioning, you have to understand the sequence of events that causes pain.

Pain is felt, as contact is made with a solid object, because the nerve endings which reach to the surface of the skin, when abused, send back signals to the brain. The intensity of pain does not depend on nerve damage, but rather on the rate of injury. Although pain does not in itself measure the severity of damage, it does indicate the speed with which injury is occurring and the rapidity required for preventive action. For the karate student, fear of injury is a natural response that creates a mental barrier which, when translated by the brain, causes an indecisive attitude at impact. This inherent apprehension of pain or injury results in an interrupted flow of energy, thereby preventing focus. The purpose of conditioning the hands is to destroy the nerve ends, to allow solid contact without the interference of these pain signals. Most body cells reproduce themselves by simple cell division, but it must be kept in mind that nerve cells follow no such pattern. Once a nerve cell is destroyed, it is destroyed forever.

Developing callus between the bones and the surface of the skin is another objective in conditioning the hands. This is accomplished by constantly hitting the hands against an object set up for that purpose, such as a *maki-wara* board or a heavy bag. If an area of the skin is rubbed repeatedly, the skin will form a callus, an accumulation of hard, dead scales. Approximately twenty layers of dead scales form the surface of a callus. This acts as a shock absorber and reduces the degree of pain from contact with a hard, resistant surface.

Although there are beneficial aspects to developing the hands for breaking, you must also learn to recognize certain harmful conditions that may arise in order to avoid serious

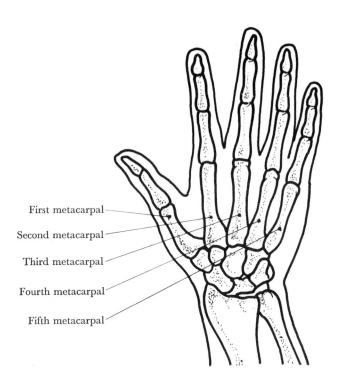

First metacarpal

Second metacarpal

Third metacarpal

Fourth metacarpal

Fifth metacarpal

The study of the hand should be a part of every student's training.

complications. One such problem is the student's overeager approach to developing calluses on the knuckles. If scar tissue is formed too quickly, it can impede finger movement by strangling the tendon that controls its mobility. Besides causing pain, it may require surgery to free the tendon to perform its proper function.

Another affliction common to tendons is called a ganglion. This is an enclosed tumorlike lesion, localized in or about a tendon sheath or joint capsule. It is most frequently found in the hands, wrists, and feet. A ganglion forms when a herniation develops in the sheath that covers the tendon. At the point of rupture a fluid-filled lump will appear. Although ganglions are more of a nuisance than anything else, they will affect your breaking because they weaken the tendon at that spot. There are two methods used to correct this disorder, one more extreme than the other. A

Ganglion.

ganglion can sometimes be reduced in size simply by draining it through a needle, injecting a small amount of cortisone to avoid inflammation, and then immobilizing the area with pressure for a few days. However, this procedure is seldom permanently effective, and in most cases the ganglion should be removed surgically, so that the defect in the tendon sheath can be sewn up. The surgical procedure, although quite successful, may still create future distress or complications for the student.

In addition to the fractures which plague students, jammed or dislocated fingers and toes present a problem. They must be recognized and treated professionally. Although many older first-aid manuals contain detailed instructions for reducing dislocations, most authorities today agree that inexpert attempts at manipulating dislocated joints are likely to fail, and do more harm than good. The bone may be fractured as well as dislocated and any movement may cause a splintered bone to sever a nerve or tendon. If a tendon is cut, it must be repaired as soon as possible, or the finger or toe may be rendered useless. First-aid treatment should be confined to immobilizing the injured joint with padded splints. Get to a hospital or doctor as soon as possible. Time is of the essence because the longer the joint remains dislocated the greater the risk of permanent damage to nerves and tendons.

Common injuries in the martial arts are sprains and strains, sprains being the more common to the breaker. The ankle, knee, thumb, and wrist—the hard working, weight-bearing joints—are the ones most often sprained. A sprain, by definition, tears the ligaments, which are attached to the bones and hold the joint together. Thus the joint is weakened and unstable until healing occurs. In addition, there may be bleeding into the joint, and considerable swelling of the surrounding tissues along with varying degrees of pain. First-aid treatment must first support and immobilize the injured joint and minimize tissue swelling. The safest procedure to follow is to use adhesive tape or an elastic bandage to provide both pressure and support to the joint. Never make the bandage too tight, as this can cut off circulation and lead to more serious injury. To help control swelling in a sprain, ice packs should be applied to the joint for the first 24 hours after the injury. Thereafter, hot water can be used to soak the joint. Soak for 20 minutes, three or four times a day. If pain and swelling persist for more than two or three days, a physician should be consulted and X rays taken to rule out possible fracture.

While a sprain affects the ligaments of the joints, a strain is associated with the muscles. A strain usually afflicts tired, unconditioned, or overused muscles. You are more apt to get a strain if you work out when you are tired. Serious muscle strain can also occur when working on a new technique which requires jumping or twisting motions. Treat a strain with the most basic first aid. Relax in a hot tub followed by a gentle rubdown of the sore area.

In addition to the aforementioned injuries, karate students are sometimes afflicted by arthritis. This crippling inflammation of the joints is an ailment easily disregarded. Arthritis could be the after-effect of years of abusing the joints. Of course, it won't happen to everyone, but it certainly warrants concern.

■ Endurance

To excel in any area of karate, be it kata, fighting, or breaking, requires good endurance. The need for endurance is obvious in fighting and kata, but its importance for breaking is harder to explain.

In order to break, your body must produce energy. Your body's ability to produce energy depends on its oxygen supply; the level of oxygen in the body is influenced by your endurance. The energy produced will be in proportion to the oxygen consumed.

Endurance training increases the efficiency of the lungs, conditioning them to process more oxygen with the least amount of effort. In other words, endurance improves your body's ability to take in oxygen and deliver it to the tissue cells where it combines with foodstuffs and is converted to energy. Since energy production relies on a good oxygen supply, the following three exercises are listed because of their ability to increase the intake of oxygen.

Jumping rope has many advantages over other endurance-building exercises. A jump rope permits many variations in technique, is inexpensive, can be used indoors and out, and provides exercise to both arms and legs. Ten minutes of vigorous rope skipping has been found to provide the same cardiovascular benefit as 30 minutes of jogging. Maximum benefit can be gained by this exercise, by first learning the basics of rope jumping. Hold your forearms down and out at a 45-degree angle with your hands 8 to 10 inches from your hips and your upper arms near your ribs. When you bounce, come 1 inch off the floor with a slight bend at your ankles, knees, and hips. Jumping rope, in addition to its endurance-building qualities, aids the mind and body by developing coordinated movements between the arms and legs. Success in the martial arts depends to a large extent on acquiring this rudimentary skill.

Jogging is one of the better endurance-building exercises. Many detailed books have been written to aid the beginner, and are readily available at bookstores and libraries for those who want to make a comprehensive study of the subject. Some basic facts are included here so that you can comfortably start jogging. The first thing to do is buy a good pair of running shoes; sneakers will not do. Shin splints are the biggest single problem for a runner. The symptoms are tightness and pain in the muscles in the front part of the leg below the knee. They are usually caused by running on hard surfaces with hard shoes and are successfully treated by wearing cushioned shoes and running on softer surfaces. Do not run with rigid knees; bend them slightly in order to absorb some of the impact as the foot makes contact with the ground. Use the heel-to-toe method; make contact with the flat of the foot first and then roll the weight forward from the heel to the toe. A goal to aim at is an 8-minute mile.

Stationary bicycles have one advantage in bad weather: they can be used indoors. The most important thing in bike riding is to find the correct height for the seat and handle bars. If the seat is positioned either too high or too low, the leg muscles will be unable to function efficiently, and you will waste energy struggling against the bicycle. With your toe on the pedal, at full extension downward, there should be a small bend at the knee. The handle bars should be positioned so that the body is relaxed and leaning slightly forward. To achieve an endurance workout on a stationary bicycle, cycle at a speed of 15 to 20 miles per hour. For those bikes that have a tachometer instead of a speedometer, the cycling rate should be 60 to 80 revolutions per minute. A goal for stationary cycling is a 4-minute mile.

■ Meditation

Meditation is to the mind what exercise is to the physical body. Both are equally important in the study of the martial arts. The fortitude, strength, and endurance gained by exercise can be equated with the inner strength, concentration, and state of awareness gained by meditation. Concentration is, in essence, the beginning of meditation. Through concentration it is possible to temporarily withdraw from the physical world. To acquire self-mastery in this technique, one must be capable of separating oneself from a tension-filled existence.

The concentration and control demanded by the martial arts are a means of achieving spiritual as well as physical fulfillment. It has been only in the last few years that this obscure and misunderstood culture from the Orient has taken a foothold upon our shores. It is now readily acknowledged to be the key to feats hitherto thought to be beyond the physical limits of the ordinary man. The previously accepted attitude that meditation was irrelevant to one's achievements has fast fallen by the wayside. Today, even in colleges throughout the country, there are courses for credit in Yoga and meditation.

Zen, Taoism, and Yoga are all cultural philosophies that teach self-realization. From these philosophical teachings, we in the martial arts world have borrowed the principle of concentration through meditation. Meditation will allow body and mind to act as a single unit, thereby accelerating the flow of energy through the body. We may contemplate, as a meditation technique, the transitory na-

ture of this energy, traveling from the seat of its power to its point of release. The idea is to channel its incessant wanderings within the body down a directed path. Through concentration, we can change the state of our consciousness in varying degrees. The depth we hope to reach is to transcend the conscious mind to reach the subconscious. To control the unconscious thoughts, which are always present throughout a movement, is to control the total harmony between body and mind. You will then have the long sought-after uninterrupted flow of energy that will elevate your physical accomplishments.

Our accomplishments are only limited by our inability to see the barriers that restrain us. Once an obstacle is acknowledged and overcome through meditation, it is then, and only then, that we rid ourselves of fears and inhibitions. It stands to reason that, once we transcend our ignorance, our accomplishments will be exceeded only by our desires.

■ Breath Control and Kiai

Preparing for a difficult breaking technique often causes emotional tension that affects physical movement. This can result in a loss of both internal power and external flexibility. However, by remaining calm and breathing properly, you can avoid the negative effects of stress. The more relaxed you remain, the more clearly you will perceive the amount of force in a movement as well as its direction. Proper breathing is therefore an important lesson to be learned in breaking.

As the mind begins to dwell on a target, breathing, without conscious effort, will usually become deeper. When breathing becomes deeper, nerve centers, such as those located in the back and shoulders, will become tense. Because the conscious mind believes that strength can only be generated from this tense contraction of muscle, it can, unknowingly, actually impede the flow of energy in the body. As physical contraction of muscle is relied upon, through tension or conscious effort, flexibility, and with it the possibility of adjusting a movement to difficult body positions, will be lost. You must learn to coordinate breathing with movement until it becomes an unconscious reflex action. This is an essential ingredient that heightens your ability to efficiently focus energy in a given direction.

In breaking, it is essential to learn the art of smooth, effortless motion. The importance of excluding erratic movements cannot be overemphasized. Applying a technique with sharp or jerky movements can cause overcommitment in an action. Movements which are made smoothly enable you to perform an action in a natural flowing manner. As a movement flows unhindered, perception is more easily interpreted. Only when the body is moving naturally can the mind be free from tensions which hinder this power of perception. Reflexes can then flow with the spontaneity of uncalculated movement.

The mind must be conditioned not to focus attention on each movement of a break. It must only be conscious of its goal, not of any intermediary movements to reach that goal. If you do not pay particular attention to coordinating breathing with the breaking movement, tension will arise and you will become keenly aware of each pulsing motion within that movement. This distraction will continually draw you away from the psychological edge that the mind must have over any difficult break.

A common mistake, made by both the beginner in breaking as well as the advanced student learning a new technique, is to unconsciously hold in the breath at the most critical point of the break, thereby causing tension. This tension transmits shock to the muscles which will then cause the body to lose its flexibility. This not only causes excessive muscular stress along the spinal column, but also transmits this stress, in the form of rigidity, to the upper and lower extremities of the body. If the spine is tense, any resistance, such as that encountered by an object you wish to break, will cause the body to lose control and offset any movements necessary to complete the break. Relating this tension to an application of self-defense, an opponent can manipulate your body simply by controlling one of your arms or legs. As with a manikin, rigid limbs can be used as handles to push or pull the rest of the body at will.

When an untrained person inhales, the chest and shoulder muscles are drawn upward. This manner of breathing creates two physiological actions, both of which tend to dominate and hamper the body's ability to adapt itself to consistent rhythmical movement. As the large muscle groups of the chest and shoulders are drawn upward, they overbalance the upper torso, greatly reducing its vertical stability. To incorporate the concept of power into a technique, movement must remain sophisticated, allowing generated intrinsic energy to flow smoothly. This will not happen if stability is not maintained. When breath control is mastered, the body is allowed to relax and settle in a strong, flexible position.

Newcomers to breaking techniques will need to make a conscious effort to learn how to inhale and exhale correctly. This will continue until the body's mechanics adjust, and the subconscious takes over the new, corrected method of breathing. A more relaxed mental attitude which transfers to the entire flexibility of movement should arise.

The breathing process is aided by the ribs, their attached muscles, and the muscle called the diaphragm which separates the chest cavity from the abdominal cavity. The lungs, having no muscle tissue, cannot by themselves expand and contract. Instead, the inhaling and exhaling movements are caused by changes in the size of the chest cavity. The size change is brought about by the ribs and

1   2   3

the diaphragm, the most important factor in the mechanical act of breathing. The diaphragm, an arched muscle, can contract with great intensity. By concentrating on controlling this muscle, you can more easily focus the force generated by this muscle at a single point.

When heavy breathing or tension interferes with the rhythmic coordination of mind and body, the breath-control exercises on the following pages should be practiced. At all times during the inhalation and exhalation phase the diaphragm is forced downward, expanding the abdomen outward. This prevents the unconscious habit of lifting the chest and shoulders upward. The expansion of the abdomen indicates that the diaphragm is fully lowered, inflating the lungs to their fullest. The air is drawn in at a constant speed and pressure. There should be no measurable pause between intake and outlet, only a blending of motion.

| 4 | 5 | 6 |

Training
Figs. 1–3   Cross your arms in front of the body. As you raise them slowly upward, begin a simultaneous intake of air. Keep your mouth closed during the inhalation phase. Take in air through your nostrils as you slowly raise your hands over your head. Keep your mind calm, concentrating only on the sound of the incoming air. When your arms are fully extended, your lungs will have filled to capacity.

Figs. 4–6   Now separate your arms to begin a downward circular motion. Start to exhale. When you release the air, you must force it out through your mouth. The sound should be like a ball of fire coming from an imaginary furnace in the lower abdominal area. When you complete this movement, you will have expelled the air in your diaphragm and lungs. An additional sharp contraction of the stomach area, with a loud *kiai* (yell; see p. 28), will force any remaining air out of the body.

7

Kiai   Breath control, as a martial arts technique, has been adopted from various Oriental teachings. The *kiai* (yell) is a variation of this breath control. Ancient masters taught that the kiai should be sharp and loud enough to kill a bird by causing it to go into shock. Today in dojos, its purpose is to cause an opponent to hesitate and lose his train of thought. To the student of breaking, the kiai is an important phase of training, as a way to increase strength.

At the moment of impact, as a breaking technique is executed, maximum muscular contraction of the stomach area is essential. This cannot be fully achieved if there is air remaining in the diaphragm. The kiai, when developed, is the necessary factor required to force out that excess air. As the yell forces air out, further contraction of the stomach muscles becomes possible.

8

To develop the yell, stand before a candle. Exhale all the air in your lungs and diaphragm as shown on page 27 above. When you feel that all the air is expelled, you then kiai, forcing the remaining air out through your mouth. When you can extinguish the candle from a distance of 12 inches, you have relieved your stomach of unnecessary air. The yell must be loud and done simultaneously with exhaling the air. Open your mouth wide, or else you will only blow out the candle as you would blow out a match.

Fig. 7

An additional exercise to increase the force of the kiai requires the aid of an assistant. You must first exhale all the air as previously explained. The assistant then swings a two-by-four, wrapped with a towel or other cloth to prevent the skin from tearing, into your stomach. A strong kiai is essential when contact is made. As the remaining air is expelled, the additional muscle contraction will make it possible to absorb the blow without injury. The assistant must be careful not to make contact with the ribs, chest cavity, or solar plexus.

Fig. 8

■ Stretching Exercises

Flexibility of movement is probably the most important facet of effective kicking techniques, whether in breaking, fighting, or kata. While many kicking techniques appear spectacular, the secret to proficiency lies mainly in becoming more limber. The exercises included here have been chosen from over 100 variations in stretching movements. They are designed to aid the legs in becoming as pliable as possible. I could fill a volume with stretching exercises; however, these were selected because they attack the ligaments, tendons, and muscles from the angles that affect flexibility.

A stretching exercise program must be followed consistently and with some knowledge of the injuries that can result from any sudden over-stretching. For example, a sudden over-stretching of a muscle may result in its over-contraction. This not only can cause stiffness later, but may also result in muscular spasm. A muscle spasm is the shortening of a skeletal muscle with loss of the ability to relax the muscle voluntarily. If the muscle shortens beyond its limit, the contraction becomes a cramp.

Muscles are attached to the bones by strong bands of tissue called tendons. The bones which we are concerned with in stretching are those that meet in a region called a joint. The joints that are important for use in effective kicking techniques are the hip and knee joints. These represent two different types of joints, and exercises are aimed at developing their individual potential. The knee is a hinge joint which limits leverage and movement to a single plane; thus we concentrate upon the stretching of the ligaments which run behind the leg. The hip is a ball-and-socket joint which permits the greatest amount of movement in all directions; thus we have exercises designed to permit elasticity to develop from all angles.

Front Kick Stretch
Fig. 1

Place one leg up on an assistant's shoulder. Do not lift the heel of the supporting leg off the floor. If the assistant raised the leg from this point, it would push you off-balance and backward. To prevent this, the assistant grasps your uniform to keep you upright. As he inches forward to raise the leg further, bend your upper body forward until your chest touches your thigh.

2

Side Kick Stretch
Fig. 2

From a side stance place your leg on an assistant's shoulder. As you raise your leg, you must turn your toes toward the floor. While you perform the stretch, twist your upper body in the direction of the extended leg. As in the Front Kick Stretch, the chest is forced down to meet the raised leg. This brings the shorter, tighter muscles and ligaments of the lower back into play.

3

Back Kick Stretch
Fig. 3

This stretch also requires an assistant. Due to the difficulty of stretching at this angle, care must be taken not to cause a cramp or muscle spasm in the lower back. This angle affects the hamstrings of the supporting leg, as well as muscles in the lower back.

Split
Fig. 4

Bring your legs out slowly in a 180-degree spread. Always be sure to warm up your legs before attempting this stretch. A torn muscle or ligament will bring a rapid halt to your progress.

Head Between Knees
Fig. 5

First sit with your legs straight and bend your upper body forward without any help. This will stretch the areas of the lower back. Now have an assistant rock you up and down until your head goes through your legs. This extra few inches brings into play the areas in the buttocks. The body is now being stretched from the lower back down to the ankles.

Straddle Leg Stretch
Fig. 6

This exercise is designed to stretch the ligaments that run down the front of the thigh. While lying back with both shoulders on the floor, lift your back thigh. For full benefit, rock this leg until it lies flat on the floor.

4

5

6

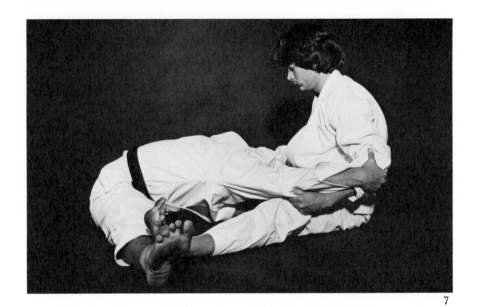

7

Leg Spread Stretch
Fig. 7

Spread your legs while in a sitting position. An assistant places his feet against the insides of your ankles. While you and he hold each other's wrists, he pushes out on your ankles. When your legs have been stretched to their maximum, he will then pull you forward to bring your head to the floor.

One-Leg Squat
Fig. 8

This is the same as a Two-Leg Squat, except for a slight variation. It is done in a wide stance and the squat is done on one leg at a time. As you alternate the stretch from side to side, be sure to come to an upright position between each squat. This will also increase the strength of the thigh muscles just above the knee.

Knee-to-Floor Stretch
Fig. 9

While in a sitting position, draw both feet into the groin. The soles of the feet touch each other. Now use your hands or elbows to press the knees down to the floor. This will stretch the areas inside the thighs up to the groin. From this position, you can bend forward to touch your head to the floor.

Straddle Front Stretch
Fig. 10

While sitting in the Straddle Leg Stretch position, bend your body forward until your head touches the front knee. This can also be done with an assistant to force the body downward an additional few inches.

1: PREPARATION FOR BREAKING · **34**

8

9   10

Hand-to-Heel Leg Stretch
Fig. 11

Sit with your right leg drawn into the groin. Hold the heel with your right hand and pull back as far as possible. The difficulty in this technique is to lock the knee while the leg is held up and back. (Repeat for left leg.)

Head-to-Knee Forward Stretch
Fig. 12

First lean backward as far as possible to stretch the ligaments up the front of the legs. Then, with the knees locked, bend your body forward to bring your head to your knees.

Leg-Raise to Floor
Fig. 13

Lie on the floor with the legs extended straight up. Now lower your legs until the toes touch the floor behind your head. Throughout this stretch, keep your knees in a locked position.

14

Squat Jump
Fig. 14   Squat Jumps are one of the best all-round leg exercises. The thrust from the floor should be as strong and as high as possible. This exercise will increase jumping height and muscular strength and will maintain flexibility of the legs while development is taking place.

PART

2 Aspects of Breaking

■ Penetration

Among the many aspects of breaking, there are three basic principles: speed, power, and penetration. Although these principles are always used in combination, one of them will dominate in each type of break you execute. We usually concentrate on speed or power in a practice break, and we should. But an equally important, though much neglected, aspect of development is penetration. Penetration is the ability to transmit the initial force of a blow through the entire movement without diminished power. Without penetration, the generated speed and power would not go beyond the first object you make contact with. Whereas the dominating principle in suspended breaks is speed, and with cement blocks power, the use of spaced boards represents the best method to gauge penetration.

Speed Break
Fig. 1

The speed of a strike must cause the shock at impact to penetrate through to the last board before the boards are pushed away. In a Speed Break the strike must be fast enough to accelerate the contact area before the sides of the boards. This bends the boards enough to break them. If the strike lacks the necessary speed, the boards will move in one mass, and they will not break.

1

2

Power Break
Fig. 2

The downward thrust of the arm must be strong enough to cause the power generated by the weight of the body to penetrate through to the last block. Therefore, the more weight you apply, the more blocks can be broken. Since the blocks offer resistance, power is the dominating principle involved.

Penetration Break
Fig. 3

The most desirable technique, representing the three requirements of breaking (speed, power, and penetration), is using boards with spaces between them. In executing this technique, the arm can reach its maximum speed without danger of injury, because of the softness and flexibility of the wood. The power generated by the weight of the body must also be at its maximum to compensate for the increasing resistance caused by the boards hitting each other as they travel downward. The key factor in this break, however, is penetration. The number of boards you are capable of breaking in this manner depends entirely on

3

your ability to maintain the speed and power of the blow until it has penetrated through to the last board. As a test of skill in penetration, place ten boards in a stack with half-inch spaces between them. Although there has been much debate on the purpose of using spaces between boards for breaking, a technique should not be prematurely judged until its rationale and degree of difficulty are perceived. The number of boards you can break, utilizing a downward strike, will indicate the depth of your penetration ability.

When working hard on breaking techniques, you should wear a wrist band or wrapping, as shown here. This serves several purposes. It protects the skin from the rough edges of the boards or blocks, and it supports the wrist, which may become weak and susceptible to injury after several breaks. In addition to the obvious physical discomfort, an injured wrist could undermine a student's self-confidence, delay training, and curtail progress for weeks.

■ Striking Points for Breaking

Palm Heel
Fig. 1

The striking area for this technique includes the fleshy part of the hand at the base of the thumb and the heel of the palm. Bend your wrist to form a 90-degree angle. Further contraction of the muscles and ligaments in this section of the hand can be obtained by curling the fingers inward to the palm.

Back Fist
Fig. 2

The same two knuckles used for the Back Fist are used later in the Forefist. The strike is made with the wrist bent inward. Because of the angle of attack, contact will be made at the top of the knuckles. This technique, whether in fighting or breaking, utilizes a snapping rather than thrusting motion.

Ridge Hand
Fig. 3

Hold your four fingers firmly together. Bend them slightly downward to increase the muscular contraction of the hand muscles. Pull the thumb into the palm to ensure that only the area around the knuckles of the forefinger will make contact.

Thumb
Fig. 4

The thumb, although rarely used, can be made into an effective weapon. It must first be strengthened before using it for breaking. It can then be used with accuracy and power, as an attacking weapon to the temple or throat, as well as other vital areas of the body.

Knife Hand
Fig. 5

To contract the muscles on the edge and heel of the palm, curl your thumb inward and bend your fingers slightly. Pay particular attention to tensing the little finger. With the exception of attacking the neck or collarbone area, the Knife Hand is used mainly for blocking. However, in breaking, this technique is utilized second only to the Reverse Punch.

Elbow
Fig. 6

The elbow is used in breaking from two different angles. The elbow joint itself must not be used when contact is made with a solid object. Due to its fragile nature and position, the elbow bone could easily be splintered.

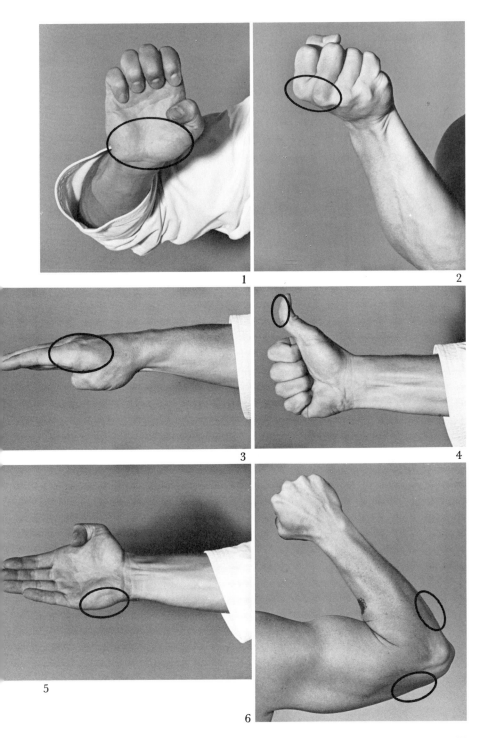

1

2

3

4

5

6

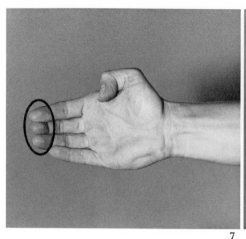 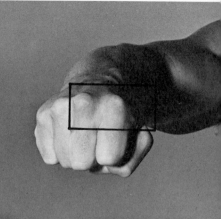

7   8

Spear Hand   The fingers must be held firmly together so they will not
Fig. 7   separate upon contact. Draw your middle finger slightly
downward to be level with the finger on each side. This
will ensure that the three finger tips involved will make
contact together.

Forefist   The Forefist is used for strikes to all parts of the body. It
Fig. 8   is snapped outward to the full extent of the arm. For
breaking, it is used against targets directly in front of the
body or in a direct downward direction. The same two
knuckles used in the Back Fist are used for the Forefist.

Ball of Foot   The toes must be curled upward as far as possible, causing
Fig. 9   the ball of the foot to project outward. For breaking,
particular emphasis is placed upon the ball directly under
the big toe. This area can be conditioned with calluses and
hardened by developing the strength of the ligaments that
are contracted by curling the toes upward.

Heel   The heel is used from two directions of attack when
Fig. 10   breaking. For Hook Kicking, the rear of the heel is used.
For Side Kicking, the side of the heel is used. Many styles
of the martial arts use the blade edge of the foot for attacking. In breaking, however, the side of the heel is least likely
to be injured upon contact.

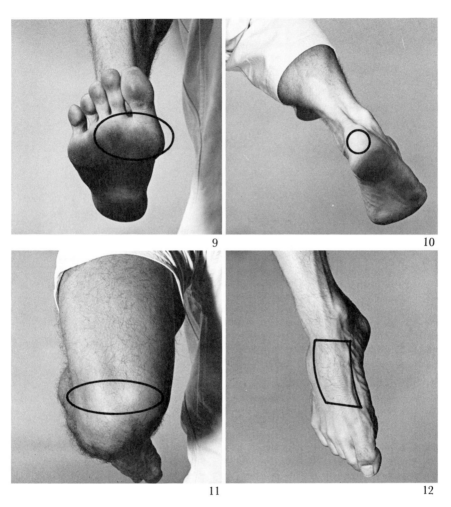

9

10

11

12

Knee
Fig. 11
Breaking with the knee must be practiced carefully to ensure that contact will be made at the right angle. The area used for contact is located approximately 2 inches above the knee cap itself. Contact with the knee cap must be avoided as the latter is only a thin shell of bone. It has no strength and is used only to protect the ligaments and cartilages connecting the knee joint.

Instep
Fig. 12
The instep, another fragile area, must be used with caution when breaking. The harder the toes are curled downward, the stronger the instep area will become. This is due to the stretching and contraction of the ligaments that run along the front of the foot.

■ The Candle

In order to progress in breaking, a speed- or strength-developing technique must be practiced daily. There are many speed-developing techniques but, realizing that not everyone can spend hours in the dojo, I have listed below only those that can be practiced anywhere. The Candle, a simple and effective speed developer, comes first.

The principle behind extinguishing a candle is to force the air in front of the moving hand to move fast enough to put out the flame. When practicing this technique, remove the top of the uniform. This will prevent the sleeves from causing turbulence in the still air.

The candles used in these pictures are five-eighths of an inch thick. This size is fairly easy to extinguish with the three hand strikes listed. However, as one candle becomes easy to put out, add a second one directly behind the first, and so on. By this procedure, you will be able to judge your progress in speed development. Another method to indicate progress is to increase the diameter of the candle. While this procedure has merit, it is more difficult to put out three or four flames than to extinguish a candle of increased diameter. Practice both methods to determine which one is more beneficial to your training. In this way you will be forced to work harder to develop the speed required.

Reverse Punch
Figs. 1–3

Line up the fist approximately two inches from the candle. This is where the striking hand will stop. Do not strike above the candle or flame.

A properly thrown punch comes from the position shown in Figure 2. The fist is well back on the hip. The hips are back, ready to spring forward. Strike directly in front of the candle using a thrust rather than a snapping punch. The snapping movement causes turbulence in the air, whereas the thrust pushes the air before it to extinguish the flame.

1

2

3

5

4

6

Knife Hand
Figs. 4–6

The Knife Hand is lined up from the side of the candles. The edge of the open hand stops directly in front of the first candle. Be sure the hand does not go above and past the first flame, for this will extinguish the candle as a fan would, not with true speed.

A properly thrown Knife Hand comes from the position shown in Figure 5. The hand is up and well back of the ear. Hips are back and ready to pivot forward. When executed with proper speed and direction, the Knife Hand will extinguish the flames as quickly as shown here. Start with one candle to learn the technique. You will find your speed and control will increase within minutes.

**Back Fist
Strike**
Figs. 7–9

The Back Fist Strike is the easiest of the hand techniques listed here. Line up the fist to the candles.

A properly thrown Back Fist comes from the position shown in Figure 8. Turn the body to the side in a strong back stance. The hand is held at the opposite ear. To extinguish two to four candles with the Back Fist technique requires a well-developed snap at the wrist. The snap is what makes the Back Fist an effective weapon of the martial arts.

10   11

Front Kick *Fig. 10*	When practicing with the Front Kick, do not hold the candle too high. Otherwise, the air moved by the kick will not push directly into the flame. Practice as low as necessary to first develop the technique for speed.
Roundhouse Kick *Fig. 11*	The Roundhouse Kick can be practiced at different heights. The higher the candle is held, the more difficult it is to extinguish the flame.
Spinning Back-Hook Kick *Fig. 12*	The Spinning Back-Hook Kick does not stop in front of the candle as in the other techniques. The foot is allowed to travel over and past the flame to extinguish it. This technique is excellent for developing control as well as speed.

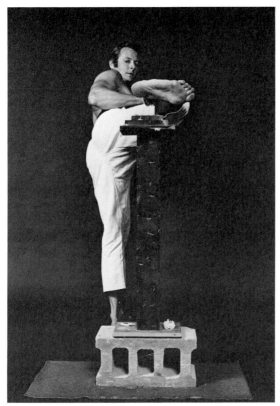

12

■ The Paper Cut

In theory the karate punch works much the same as the U.S. Army M-16 rifle. When a bullet is discharged from the rifle, it twists as it travels through the air. As the projectile makes contact, it twists and tumbles, tearing the skin and shattering any bone in its path. Hypothetically, if the bullet were to hit the ankle, it could shatter the bone up to the hip, sending the body into shock, and ultimately causing death. The karate punch, though not to be compared in power, works on the same principle. The purpose of twisting the hand in the final tenth of a second is to tear the skin and shatter the bone.

Exercises or training methods to practice and perfect this twisting effect are unfortunately limited. Most methods

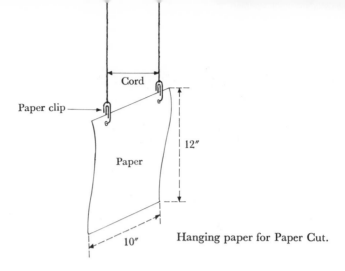

Hanging paper for Paper Cut.

used to condition the hands and practice focus require a solid or heavy object. This negates the twisting effect of the hand. In all probability, if a surface is too hard, the skin will tear on your knuckles. Since the timing of the twist must be coordinated with contact, the object used must afford some resilience. It must freely move from the path of the punch, yet still give clear evidence that the twisting of the knuckles has accomplished its purpose.

For this purpose, the Paper Cut, although extremely difficult, is probably the best indicator. To successfully tear a piece of paper suspended in air not only requires great speed, but can only be done by twisting the knuckles into the paper. If the knuckles are twisted a fraction of a second too soon or too late, the paper will not tear.

This technique is easy to set up and requires material that is usually found around the house. Take a 10″ × 12″ piece of paper and make two holes, one in each corner along the top of the paper. Insert a length of cord through each hole and tie it at one end, securing the other end to an overhead object. Both pieces of cord should be the same length and long enough to allow the center of the paper, once secured overhead, to be approximately chest high. To prevent the paper from constantly tearing off the cord, a paper clip can be inserted, as shown, between the paper and the cord. The paper clips also allow you to change the paper by simply removing the paper at the clips.

When practicing this technique you may develop a soreness in the wrist. This is usually indicative of weak muscles or ligaments in that area. The snapping effect alone, from twisting the hand, will strengthen the wrist.

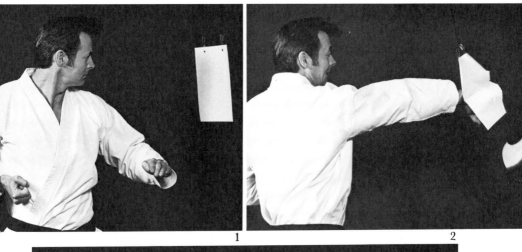

1

2

3

However, to accelerate the pace, use one of the exercises in this book designed to develop the wrist area (see p. 138).

Figs. 1–3   Because of the extreme speed necessary to successfully execute the Paper Cut, the body must remain completely relaxed throughout the movement. There must be no tension as the arm moves toward the paper. Speed should be the only thought in mind. The angle in Figure 3 shows the type of cut in the paper that will be made by the twist of the knuckles.

4

5

6

Figs. 4–6   Different techniques can also be applied to the Paper Cut. The paper is harder to cut if it is approached from different angles. The strike is correct even if the paper is not torn, provided the paper is not pushed away by the forward thrust of the movement.

■ How To Start Breaking

Before you start breaking you must understand the fundamental concept that produces the power of a karate technique. The novice, in an overzealous attempt to generate this power, very often thinks he must throw his shoulders into the punch. He will lean forward, off-balance, in a vain attempt to push his body weight into the movement. Leaning forward results in the proper distribution of body weight in the stance being unevenly shifted. Once the stance is disturbed (off-balance), the hip, stomach muscles, and thighs (the core of a karateka's power) cannot be effectively utilized. This error, throwing the shoulders forward, and the chain of faults it produces, can only be corrected by knowledge and training.

The major power generated into a movement is produced by shifting the hips forward, in perfect balance, as the technique is executed. The speed with which the lower torso is shifted is an element of training that must enter into the student's exercise program. The abdominal muscles located on the sides of the stomach, especially the external oblique abdominals, must be fully developed, as they aid in pulling the hips forward. The upper thigh muscles must be strong and powerful, as they aid in pushing the hips forward. The hip itself must be continually rotated back and forth to stretch the thick ligaments and tendons around the joint. Although developed individually, each of these areas must be unified to act as a single moving unit. Once mastered, the potential of a karate movement becomes devastating.

When ready to advance to an actual break, it is best to start, as a beginner, on an object that you know will break easily. The initial objective in breaking is to develop confidence. As your confidence grows, so will your breaking skill. Advanced techniques should be avoided, as they will only serve to discourage and dishearten you. Worse yet, by trying breaks beyond your capabilities, you might seriously injure yourself and set your progress back even further. Beginners rarely realize their limitations and often become overanxious when they see a good technique executed. Irreparable damage can be done to one's confidence by advancing prematurely. If you have doubts, you will hesitate and hold back at the moment of impact. When this happens, the energy generated within your body will dissipate and power will be lost.

Choose a simple technique and start with one board. Continue practicing the same technique until you are sure that you have the power and confidence to break that one board at will. You may then advance to two boards, and so on. Do not rush your progress. The objective in the beginning is to develop confidence and power, not to set records.

■ Wood Breaking

Wood for board breaking must be selected carefully. The texture of the wood, which is determined by the quality of the grain, has a great influence on the ease with which the boards will break. Wood can be purchased in various grains, ranging from the hard woods which have a tight grain to the softer woods which have a wide grain. For breaking, the grain should be as wide as possible and run at right angles to the cut of the wood. Wider grain allows the board to bend more readily. As the board bends, the fibers on the bottom of the wood pull apart, causing the boards to break with relative ease. The thicker the board or the tighter the grain, the less flexibility the wood will have, causing greater difficulty in breaking. By using a fairly soft wood with a wide grain, the student can make contact without fear of injury, and still measure breaking ability by increasing the number of boards.

The kind of wood normally used is clear pine shelving. A clear pine board is appropriately soft and has a wide, straight grain that is easily discernible. Be sure to examine the wood to make sure there are no knots to resist splitting. The board is usually three-quarters of an inch thick, 10 inches wide, and 12 inches long. It is important to note that, although this wood really measures three-quarters of an inch thick, when ordering from the lumber yard, you ask for a 1-inch thickness. The lumber business never uses exact measurements.

Lumber yards, as a rule, rarely sell wood in odd-length footage. To minimize waste, 6-foot lengths are the most practical. This yields seven 10-inch boards with only a

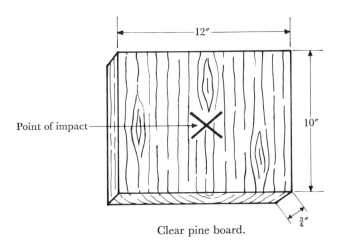

Clear pine board.

2-inch waste. It is not advisable to cut the wood until a day or two before using it. Pre-cut pieces have a tendency to dry out and crack, rendering them useless for practice.

When you set boards on supports for downward strikes, the wood must be placed to allow the break to run parallel with the grain. The width (cut side) of the board is resting upon supports, in from the edge of the board no more than one-half inch. When preparing to break, the mind must concentrate on the underside of the board where the initial separation of wood fibers begins. If the boards have a bow in them, it is always placed upward or outward. This affects the degree it will bend before breaking.

Fig. 1
(p. 60) Different methods of stacking boards present various degrees of difficulty in breaking. Although resistance is least when the boards are spaced apart, the hand must be fast enough to cause the shock from the blow to penetrate through to the last board.

Fig. 2 More resistance is created when some of the boards touch each other. Therefore, in addition to speed and penetration, power must now be generated into the strike to a greater degree.

Fig. 3 When all the boards are touching, resistance is increased in direct proportion to the number of boards being broken. Therefore, the total force and energy is multiplied by the number of boards in the same way the resistance was multiplied.

1. Least resistance.

2. More resistance.

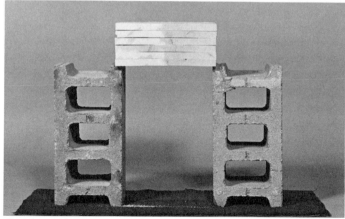

3. Most resistance.

■ The Breaker's Assistants

Fig. 1
(two views)

To ensure an effective break, assistants must also know what is important to make the break successful. An inexperienced holder may flinch, pull back, or even drop the boards. When you use only one assistant, have him hold the boards with one hand on top and the other hand on the bottom. His hands are placed on the boards at dead center. His bottom arm is bent to allow it to rest against the rib and chest area under the armpit. His upper arm is held straight out with the elbow locked. This will allow the shock from the blow to be absorbed in a straight line from the wrist to the shoulder.

1   1'

2   2′

Fig. 2   When attempting more than two boards, it is best to use
(two views)   two assistants. This prevents the sides of the boards from
moving backward, which would cause the force of the blow
to spread from its central point of focus. The outside arms
of the assistants are bent and resting against the rib and
chest area under the armpit. The inside arms are locked at
the elbow. The heels of the palms are braced behind the
boards to give resistance to the backward thrust created by
the blow. The only parts of the fingers extending over the
front of the boards are the tips. An experienced holder will
realize that even the full impact on the finger tips from a
strong side kick will not break them. The finger tips may
be flattened, turn white, and become numb from a solid
blow, but they are rarely broken.

Figs. 3, 4   When assistants must hold heavy objects, such as cement
or cinder blocks, they will need additional assistance. Another assistant is placed on each side. Their outside hands

3

4

hold the holders' bottom wrists and their inside hands hold
the holders' top wrists. In addition to absorbing some of
the weight of the objects, they also give support to the
holders' wrists. A fifth assistant may be used to apply his
body weight in a forward direction, thus preventing the
front holders from sliding backward under pressure from
the blow. The front holders must have their inside legs
back and their outside legs forward. In addition to allowing

5   6

the holders to lean against each other for added support,
this placement of legs allows the breaker to travel through
the break, without fear of landing on someone's knee or foot.

Safety precautions should never be neglected. When you
hold objects that may break and scatter into many pieces,
such as cinder blocks, you must protect your feet. Do this
Fig. 5 by arranging pre-cut boards over the foot area, protecting
the fragile instep bone and metatarsal bones, which would
be exposed to falling pieces of broken blocks.

The holder must protect his face when his partner prac-
tices techniques, especially kicks, in an upward angle to the
groin. Very often, pieces of wood from the center of the
boards fly upward, hitting the assistant in the nose, mouth,
Fig. 6 or eyes. A second assistant should place his hands over the
holder's shoulder to deflect any pieces flying toward the
face.

■ Breaking for Women

Women in karate exist in a rather limited sphere. Although many women participate in the martial arts, they are far out-numbered by their male counterparts. This, plus the fact that men are stronger (women have fewer muscles and generally weigh less) and as a rule more aggressive, often hampers the proper development of women in the art.

Karate schools, from a women's point of view, can generally be divided into three categories: those that pamper, those that abuse, and those that fall somewhere in between. Almost all teach women and men the same techniques and kata; few take into account the physical differences between the sexes. Therefore, women are often left in limbo. They have the ability and knowledge, but many times they do not have the physical strength to effectively use techniques in a street situation.

Unfortunately there are far too many women who have no chance to fight or break in self-defense schools. Participation is limited to class exercises. These women are not aware of the strength they must exert until they actually have to use it. This provides a false sense of confidence because their techniques are rarely effective. It is for this reason that I have developed a training program in breaking that women can effectively use to parallel self-defense techniques.

Palm Heel
Figs. 1–3
(See p. 119)

The Palm Heel, probably a woman's most powerful hand weapon, should only be used against the underside of an opponent's nose in an upward direction. This area of the face is extremely sensitive. Even if the strike is not properly thrown, due to nervousness or poor balance, the attacker's eyes will still fill with tears from the blow. Extreme pain will make him hesitate to regain his composure and train of thought. This split second is all you need to escape or follow-up in a counterattack.

Fig. 4

TRAINING: Put a chalk mark at the center of the boards to represent the small area of contact presented by the underside of the nose. Then, if you make contact with the small area being aimed at, it will leave a chalk mark on your hand.

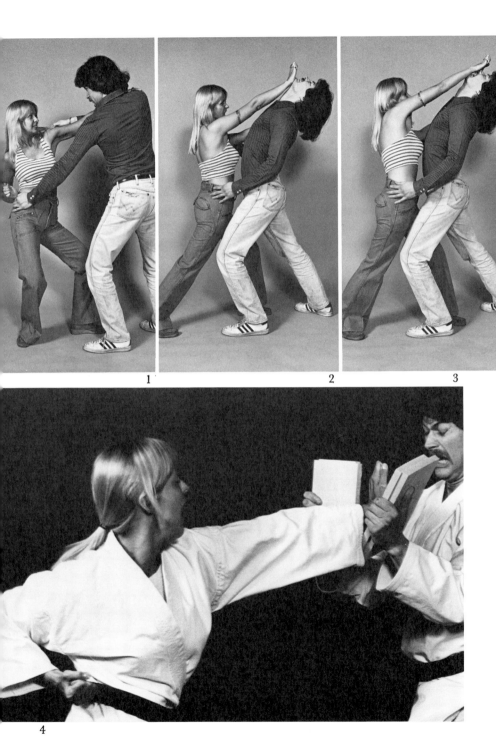

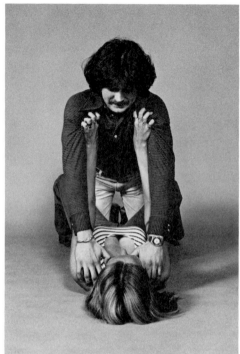

5

6

Spear Hand
Figs. 5–7
(See p. 136)

The Spear Hand, which utilizes a woman's finger nails, can easily blind an attacker. This technique is only recommended for use in the most serious cases, such as rape attempts. Do not put a person's eye out for grabbing a purse or pocketbook. For a woman, the greatest obstacle to self-defense is the inability to inflict injury to an attacker's vital areas. Revulsion is usually the primary reason for this. It must be overcome through training, as it blocks a woman's most basic pathway to survival.

Fig. 8

TRAINING: Exercises, such as thrusting the hand into a watermelon, are designed to develop thrust, increase accuracy, and overcome inhibition. Although messy, when executed properly, it helps subdue self-conscious feelings of looking unfeminine. Such feelings have no place in a self-defense program if there is an honest desire to progress.

2: ASPECTS OF BREAKING • **68**

7

8

9 10

Hammer Fist
Figs. 9–11
(See p. 128)

In this grab from behind, the attacker places one arm around your neck to hold you, while he reaches with his other hand. This position leaves one of your arms free to be used as a weapon. Under these circumstances, the most advantageous area to attack would be the groin. As you raise your right hand high to gain downward momentum, move your right leg back between the attacker's legs. This backward movement places the entire weight of the body behind the strike. Effective use of body weight, especially for a woman, may mean the difference between an effective technique and failure—or between life and death.

TRAINING: This technique is difficult to master because it requires accuracy and precise timing. To augment the force behind the blow, as well as to see the target better,

Fig. 12

twist the hips and upper body slightly in the direction of the strike at the moment of impact. When performed correctly, this move capitalizes on the strength of the arm, shoulder, and hip.

13   14

Instep to Groin
Figs. 13–15
(See p. 165)

The distance between you and the attacker will determine the direction of counterattack, as well as the type of strike used. Instantaneous response is essential in a street situation. Quickening your response time and reflex actions should be primary objectives when practicing. In this particular case, as you pivot to face the attacker, you should be in a strong kicking stance. Then thrust your leg between the attacker's legs. This area of contact, from the instep up to the shin, is 12 inches long, enough to allow a deep penetration to the groin. If you were to aim at the groin with the ball of the foot, the attacker would only have to flinch 2 inches, and you would miss your target completely.

Fig. 16

TRAINING: In practice, a protective covering should be used to cushion the instep bone. The purpose of breaking with this technique is to feel the proper angle of attack and to develop increased leg power. Psychologically, breaking forms the foundation that strong self-confidence is built on.

2: ASPECTS OF BREAKING · **72**

15

16

17   18

Elbow Strike   The Elbow Strike, when used in a situation where you
Figs. 17–19   are grabbed from behind, is usually directed at the ribs.
(See p. 106)   Keep in mind that an attacker has, with clothing, skin,
muscle, and fat, a substantial cushion to absorb a blow to
that area. A cushion of only two inches would be enough
to dissipate the focus and negate the power of anyone's
elbow strike. This strike, however, would be effective if
directed against the back of the jaw, dislocating the jawbone
where it hinges onto the skull. Minimum effort is required,
provided you are accurate in your point of contact.

TRAINING: Twist the upper body into the strike with
speed and determination. You can learn this, when break-
Fig. 20   ing, by practicing the Elbow Strike from all directions.
Women, generally weighing less than men, must train to
deliver every pound into a strike. Since vital areas are
difficult targets, considering their small size and limited
locations, accuracy is essential.

19

20

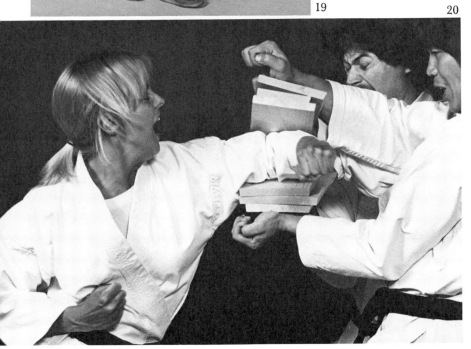

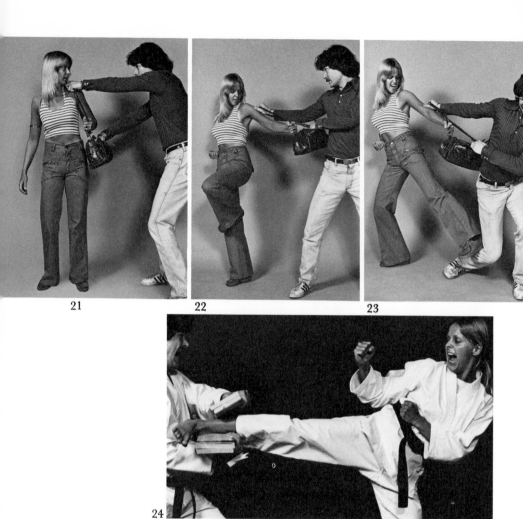

21   22   23

24

Side Kick
Figs. 21–23
(See p. 171)

The Side Kick, although one of the strongest techniques, still has only limited effectiveness against an advancing assailant. Therefore, a woman must be capable of directing her counterattack to an attacker's weaker points. In this case, she compensates by delivering a strike to the side of the knee, easily incapacitating the provoker.

Fig. 24

TRAINING: The main purpose of breaking with this technique is to coordinate the pivot of the stationary leg with the forward thrust of the hips. This combination of movements must be continually practiced to become a perfectly unified motion as the body thrusts forward to meet its objective.

2: ASPECTS OF BREAKING · **76**

Breaking:
Hand Techniques

■ Reverse Punch

The Reverse Punch emanates both speed and power. Spectators, easily awed by this power in motion, sit spellbound by the seemingly magical force which enables men to smash bricks, tiles, or cement blocks barehanded. Much of the aura surrounding this punch is a product of the current film market and promotional agencies in the martial arts, but the Reverse Punch is, nevertheless, the most devastating of the hand-strike techniques.

The well-trained student knows that the key to mastering this punch is knowledge—knowledge of one's anatomy, one's mind, and, most important, one's confidence. To act without full control of any of these elements is just so much wasted effort.

The Reverse Punch utilizes the greatest tool of the human body, the hand. Of the 206 bones in the human skeleton, 8 are in the wrist, 5 in the palm, and 14 in the fingers on each hand. With proper dedication and training, this tool can be molded into a formidable weapon. In the execution of the punch, the mind and body must be in perfect co-ordination, synchronized to act as one. The need for this is apparent; with the adjustment in proper order, more than 30 joints and 50 muscles of the hand, wrist, arm, and shoulder are brought into play.

As mentioned in other areas of this text, successful utilization of a body part to break a solid object must be preceded by a full understanding of the abilities and limitations of that anatomical area. Comprehension of the physical design of the hand is essential if the Reverse Punch is to be done with precision and without injury.

Students are taught to make a fist by first curling the tips of the fingers into the palm. This will give the second and third knuckles, the contact area, the support of the thenar eminence, which provides an almost rigid support to the wrist. The thumb is curled over the index and middle fingers to reinforce this support. The fourth and fifth metacarpals are supported at an angle with no direct support to the wrist and, for this reason, are never used to make contact. Sufficient pressure can cause a fracture or dislocation of these knuckles.

All fingers, when making a fist, are controlled by a set

of fibers called tendons. Like pulley cords, these tendons run from the hand to muscles which control them. Although some of the muscles are located in the palm itself, most are in the forearm. Avoid using tight wrist wraps when practicing, as they tend to tire the hand by restricting the tendons. Wrist wraps, used when breaking, should be secure, not tight.

In practice, the Reverse Punch is done slowly. Each muscle within that group of controlling muscles must be tensed throughout the entire extension of the arm. The shoulder must remain back and level. If the shoulder is raised, the chest muscles cannot be fully contracted. The elbow remains close to the body after the outward thrust of the arm in order to maintain its direct line behind the wrist as it moves toward the target. The hips are snapped into a twisting motion in the direction of the target to increase the momentum of the punch. The back leg is locked at the knee with the rear foot pressing into the floor.

Every movement in karate has as a common denominator the law of physics, "To every action there is an opposite and equal reaction." In the Reverse Punch this is especially true because the greater the force and speed with which the opposite hand is retracted, the greater the force and speed of the punching hand. In the last tenth of a second, the fist is snapped into a locked position, increasing the force and speed of the blow.

An imaginary point directly in front of the center of the body, approximately opposite the heart, is used during practice as a target. At this point, the greatest number of muscles are used, thereby concentrating the greatest amount of strength in that area. When the fist is directed and moved toward this point, it will be moving the shortest distance for full extension of the arm. The fist is then moving, from its starting point at the hip to its finishing point at the target, at the greatest possible speed across the shortest possible distance.

Fractures of the hand or knuckle are common but in most cases preventable. The need to line up the knuckles to the target is essential. The proper movement and coordination is mandatory; synchronization of body and mind is indispensable; and prematurely exceeding one's capacity is taboo.

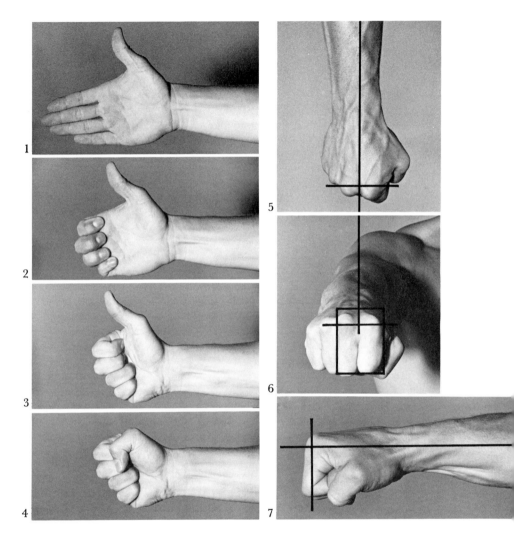

Forefist
Figs. 1–4   The fist is probably the most widely used part of the body for breaking. It is of utmost importance that it be held properly. Therefore, when curling the fingers into the palm to make a fist, place particular emphasis on the knuckles of the forefinger and middle finger, which absorb the entire shock of the blow. The thumb does not make contact, although it does serve an equally important function. It must be tightly curled over the forefinger and middle finger to prevent them from jarring loose upon contact.

Figs. 5–7   The horizontal line, drawn from the knuckles to the shoulder, simulates the shock wave created by a blow as

REVERSE PUNCH · **81**

it travels back along this line and rapidly loses force. If on contact, any part of this imaginary line is not straight, the shock wave will travel back to the deviation and stop. Unable to diminish naturally, the pressure will build to the point of causing possible injury. Common injuries include dislocated elbows, from making contact before the elbow is locked, and broken wrists, caused by bending the wrist joint on contact. It cannot be overemphasized that the shock wave must be allowed to flow without meeting any resistance.

Punching Stance

Although the punch can be practiced from many stances, for breaking purposes we are only concerned with the Back Stance. To fully utilize body weight behind the punch, the hip and pelvic movement must be coordinated with the forward thrust of the arm. This demands exact timing, since the hips move a fraction of a second ahead of the hand. The Back Stance affords us the opportunity to employ this forward thrust to its maximum.

The Back Stance, when used in breaking, varies slightly from the Traditional Back Stance in the placement of the feet. The feet are placed at a 90-degree angle for the Traditional Back Stance. The heels are directly in line with each other to allow for smooth forward and backward movement. For breaking, the front foot is placed out the same distance. However, it is not aligned with the rear foot but is placed approximately 8 inches to the left. This placement allows for the proper shift of weight as the body pivots into the direction of the punch.

Figs. 8, 9

In the Back Stance, the rear leg supports 70 percent of the body weight, and the front leg supports the remaining 30 percent. As the punch is delivered to its objective, the rear foot pivots. This pivot thrusts the hips forward, bringing the body to a forward position. Forty percent of the weight distribution is now on the rear foot and 60 percent on the front. This forward thrust has transferred 30 percent

Figs. 10, 11

of the body weight from the rear to the front leg, as can be seen in Figures 10 and 11. For instance, a 150-pound student, pivoting from the Back Stance to the Front Stance, will thrust an additional 45 pounds of body weight behind the punch.

Traditional Back Stance.   Variation for breaking.   Pivot the rear foot.

30°
90°

8

9

10

11

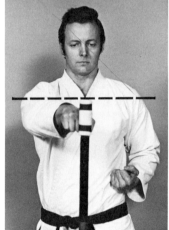

Approach	When you face the target, your left shoulder is at a 45-
Fig. 12	degree angle. The toes of your rear foot are on a 90-degree angle. Your upper body is on a vertical line with the heel of your rear foot.
	Pivot the toes of your rear foot to a 30-degree angle to the front. Move your shoulders from the 45-degree angle to a
Fig. 13	squared horizontal position. Keep your upper body straight and perpendicular to the floor. Shift your center of gravity forward, centered between both legs in perfect balance.
Fig. 14	Thrust your body forward by pivoting on the ball of the rear foot. Do not lift your heel off the floor; you must shift it along the ground.

3: BREAKING: HAND TECHNIQUES • **84**

16 17 18 19

Fig. 15

When moving from the Back to the Front Stance, keep your hips and shoulders on a level plane throughout the movement.

Strike
Figs. 16–19

Movement of feet, hips, and shoulders must be perfectly synchronized with the forward thrust of the arm. As your hand moves from the hip, it remains close to the side of the body. Your elbow must remain directly behind the wrist from the beginning to the end of the movement. With your arm fully extended, contract the forearm muscles to add power to the twisting of the wrist. In the last tenth of a second, twist your hand into the target. The entire body, especially the shoulder of the punching arm, must remain relaxed while in motion. Tension will slow the uncoiling action of the moving arm. The muscles of the body are fully contracted only at the moment of impact. You must press the heel of your rear foot into the floor with the knee locked. This allows a straight path for the flow of energy to travel— from floor, to hips, to arm.

20   21   22

23. Wrong.

Figs. 20–23   If you allow the elbow to move away from the body and arc outward, it will prevent focus and cause the arm to collapse upon impact.

Pointers   The twisting motion of the hips as they are thrust for-
Figs. 24, 25   ward, combined with the speed of the punching arm (approximately 10 mph), accumulates the energy at the point of focus. The arm must follow through to its full extension along a straight line. This is essential to transmit the power generated by the transfer of weight distribution as the stance shifts forward.

24

25

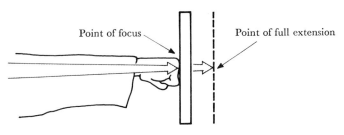

The arm follows through the break.

26

27

Change in direction of tension.

Figs. 26, 27   To control the transfer of weight as it moves toward the target, lock your rear knee as your front knee becomes perpendicular to the toes of your foot. Note in the sketches how the angle of your rear leg changes as you pivot on the ball of your rear foot.

Variation   A variation of the Reverse Punch, used when practicing *Figs. 28–31*   alone, utilizes the downward thrust of the arm and hips. The fist is still kept close to the body. However, rather than coming from the hip, as previously shown in the Outward Thrust Punch, it is held higher and comes from the chest.

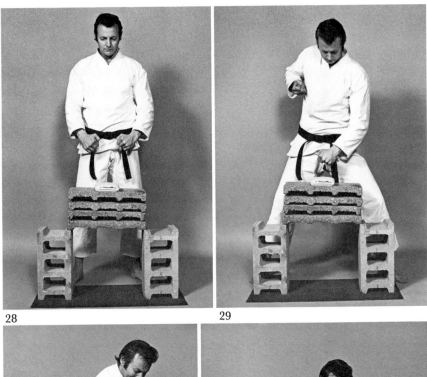

28 29

30 31

Do not pull the punch back as the object is broken. Allow your hand to continue to its full extension. Aim beyond the bottom block, and do not relax your power until the hand has gone through and beyond the material.

32. Right.   33. Wrong.

Figs. 32, 33   Although the shoulder of the punching arm is allowed to drop into the break, adding power to the downward thrust of the arm, the opposite shoulder must not move from its vertical alignment with the knee. In the wrong position the shoulder moves off the vertical line, causing the body to bend forward and wasting the power generated by the hip.

Figs. 34–36   Make contact with the knuckles of the forefinger and middle finger. The fist must be held tightly, on impact, to prevent these knuckles from being jarred loose. Fractures of the hand rarely occur from the force of a blow; they result, rather, from an improperly thrown punch or lax attitude. The ring-finger and little-finger knuckles have no direct line of support to the wrist. Therefore, they never make contact with the target. Improper form is shown in Figure 35.

3: BREAKING: HAND TECHNIQUES · **90**

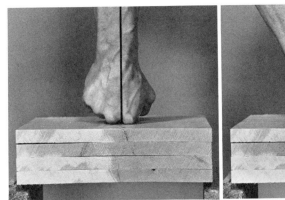
34. Right.

35. Wrong.

36

37

38

39

40

41

42

Application
Figs. 37–42
As different areas of an attacker's body become vulnerable to counterattack, you must be quick to capitalize on your opponent's mistakes. An important aspect of the counterattack is to counter at the same height as the attack. In other words, if the attack is high, counter high, and likewise, if the attack is low, counter low. This attitude frees your mind of decision making, allowing your concentration to remain on one level. Instantaneous reflex action is a product of the coordinated mind and body.

■ Knife Hand

The Shuto or Knife Hand is second only to the Reverse Punch as an important hand strike. Its use is stressed, without exception, in all styles of the martial arts. Because of its universal use and popularity, the knife edge of the hand is explained in detail.

The meaty section of the palm, and the corner section of the palm heel where it joins the wrist, constitute the knife edge of the hand. Some controversy exists about the inclusion of the palm heel, but for the purpose of breaking, it is mandatory to include both sections.

The heel of the palm, although small in area, contains eight bones. The pisiform bone is the one we are directly concerned with when breaking. A small bone on the inner and anterior aspect of the wrist, it is about the size and shape of a half pea. Breaking with the Knife Hand exposes the ulnar artery and ulnar nerve, located in close proximity to this bone, to great danger. If the pisiform bone is smashed or fractured, bone splinters in the area of the artery and nerve can cause serious problems. For this reason, you must strengthen this section of the hand by developing calluses. The thicker the callus formed on the heel of the palm, the greater the shock absorbency between the surface and the pisiform bone. You can easily harden this area by using either a *makiwara* board or a heavy bag.

One section of the hand should not make contact during breaking—the knuckle bone of the little finger. This, the fifth metacarpal, has a high incidence of knuckle fracture. Although it is not the most slender of the metacarpals, the cortex of this knuckle is usually the thinnest of the five. To prevent contact, you must align your hand at the proper angle.

Raise your hand well above the shoulder and swing into the target. As your arm approaches the surface, twist your hand slightly inward and pull toward the body just before impact. This twisting effect has a twofold purpose: to force contraction of the hand muscles and to increase the speed of the blow. The angle of the hand upon contact should be such that the tip of the little finger is approximately 1 inch above the surface of the object. The shock of the blow will rapidly pull the little finger toward the object. This will cause sharp pain, or even break the finger, if the angle is incorrect when hand and object connect. Until you master this technique, alignment of hand and target cannot be overemphasized.

Muscular contraction upon contact is essential in the Knife Hand, as in all karate techniques. To insure this, curl your thumb tightly into the palm and slightly bend the remaining fingers. This allows complete tension in the entire hand, especially the striking area that will make contact. The finger-tip push-ups mentioned on page 138 are fundamental to strengthen the muscles of the hand. Powerful hand strikes depend on developing strong fingers and grip.

Form
Figs. 1–4
(two views)

From the hip, raise your hand immediately to a position above the shoulder. Keep your elbow parallel to the floor. Hold your hand near your ear with the palm facing forward. As your hand starts its strike toward the target, it begins to twist with a snap at the wrist. The hand travels in a slight downward arc from the ear to the point of contact.

The snapping effect of the elbow combined with the twisting of the wrist increases the force and speed of the blow. You must keep your elbow bent as you make contact to lessen the shock to the joint itself. Hold the fingers firmly together to prevent them from separating on impact. When practicing, stop the strike at an imaginary line in front of the body.

Side view. 1 2 3 4

Front view. 1' 2' 3' 4'

KNIFE HAND · **95**

5. Concentrate.   6. Prepare.

Strike
Figs. 5–9

Assume a stance in front of the target. You will need a few seconds of mental concentration to separate the mind from surrounding noises. Some people gaze into space while others appear to stare through the object. You must unite the mind and body with the one goal of accomplishing the break. Raise your hand high above the shoulder and swing with great speed into the target. Upon impact, lower your stance to pull the hand through the target. The arm continues through the break until the stance has locked onto its final position.

Practice

There are two distinct methods to increase one's breaking ability, each with separate goals. The first and more common of these methods slowly augments the difficulty of the break to correspond with the student's strength. This is accomplished by increasing either the thickness or the number of pieces of the breaking material. However, the other method used, as illustrated for the Knife Hand break,

7. Strike.

8. Break.

9. Final position.

10	11
12	13

Figs. 10–13   serves to strengthen the student's ambidexterity. Notice that the model has successfully accomplished this break simultaneously with both hands. This was done with equal amounts of strength, timing, and coordination. To achieve peak perfection, it is necessary to develop these qualities on both sides of the body. Do not neglect the weaker side, as so many students are apt to do. It is essential that all breaks be practiced with both arms or legs and with a consistent rate of development so that the body can develop to its greatest capacity.

14

15

Figs. 14, 15   The Knife Hand Strike should be practiced from every conceivable angle. Most students of the art prefer to use techniques that will employ their strike from the strongest direction. Although this is acceptable in practice, it is not practical if you are caught off-guard in a street situation. Many of the weaker striking techniques are completely overlooked, probably because their effectiveness is underestimated. The true practitioner of the art learns to make use of every part of the body from head to heel, and from every angle.

Breaking a Free-Standing Target
Figs. 16–18

When breaking a free-standing target, the arm must travel at great speed. As the hand makes contact, the entire muscular system of the body is tensed and then instantly relaxed. This tension is exerted on the target for only a few seconds before following through on the technique. Timing must be precise so as not to exert too much pressure. Excess pressure would merely push the target away from the moving arm.

Pointers
Fig. 19
Fig. 20
(two views)

When you perform the Knife Hand Strike from a high angle, as when attacking the collarbone, you must begin your strike with a greater degree of speed. Because the downward distance the hand travels is shorter, less body weight is utilized.

Fig. 21
Fig. 22
(two views)

The angle of this strike also requires that speed be the dominating factor. Since the movement is horizontal rather than vertical, fewer shoulder and chest muscles are used.

19

21

20

22

20'

22'

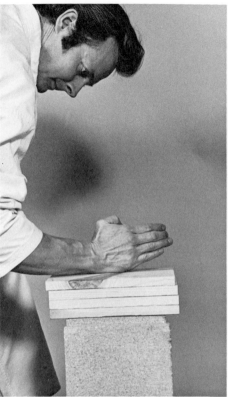

23   23'

Fig. 23	Proper concentration and hand alignment are essential to
(two views)	instill confidence and prevent injury.
Fig. 24	From the speed of the movement, the little finger will

Fig. 23
(two views)
Proper concentration and hand alignment are essential to instill confidence and prevent injury.

Fig. 24
From the speed of the movement, the little finger will be pulled toward the surface of the break. If the angle of the hand is correct as impact is made, the broken material will be traveling away from the finger. This will prevent contact of the finger with the surface.

Fig. 25
If the thumb comes out of its tucked position, less tension is on the knife-edge side of the hand. This will adversely affect the break. The tighter the thumb is curled inside, the more the hand and finger muscles can contract.

24

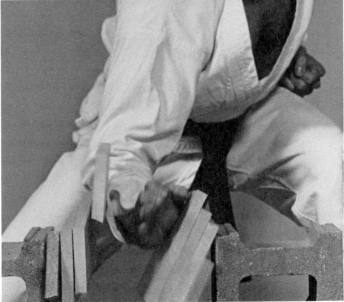

25. Wrong.

26

Application
Figs. 26–32   The angle of the counterattack should be determined as the assailant moves within your striking range. Once you make contact with your assailant, maximum contraction is essential to focus through layers of protective covering.

3: BREAKING: HAND TECHNIQUES • **104**

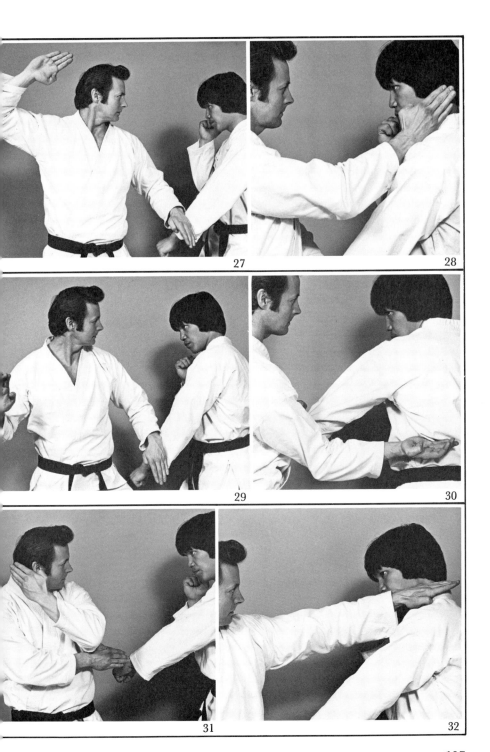

27

28

29

30

31

32

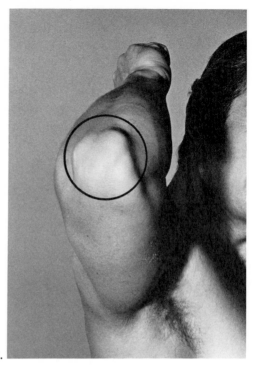

1. Elbow joint.

■ Elbow Strike

Fig. 1

The Elbow Strike, as uncomplicated as it may sound, requires some explanation, both for the beginner and the advanced student. Although it is called the Elbow Strike, the elbow joint itself is not actually used because of its fragile position. The elbow cannot be conditioned, like other areas of the body, to protect it against solid blows. To do so could cause calcium deposits to develop within the joint. This painful and often debilitating condition is brought on by constantly snapping the elbow. Many great athletic careers have been abandoned as a result. Treatment to relieve the discomfort is restricted to painful injections in the joint; in more serious cases, an operation is necessary.

There are actually two different parts of the arm which can be used in the Elbow Strike, depending on which of two methods you select.

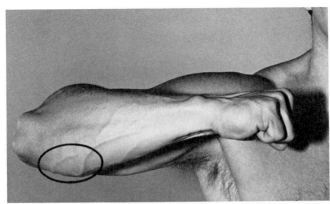

2. Area for Forward Thrust.

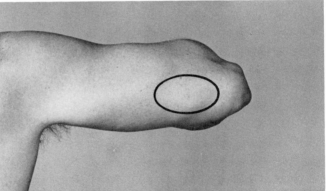

3. Area for Downward or Backward Thrust.

Fig. 2

Fig. 3

Method 1 is used against a target directly in front of you. This is called the Forward Thrust. Method 2 is called either a Downward or Backward Thrust. Figure 2 shows the part of the arm used in the Forward Thrust Elbow Strike. It is an area of approximately 3 inches starting an inch down from the joint. Figure 3 illustrates the area of the arm used in the Downward or Backward Thrust, which again is approximately 3 inches in area starting an inch up from the joint. As can be readily seen in both photos, the fist is positioned at a 90-degree angle to the elbow. This angle is extremely important to obtain maximum muscle contraction in the forearm muscles used in Method 1, and the lower triceps muscle used in Method 2. If the fist is improperly held straight up and down (palm toward shoulder), the biceps muscle, which is not used, is contracted. This substantially reduces the energy produced and released for the Elbow Strike.

4   5   6

7. Wrong.

Method 1
Figs. 4–6 Move your elbow forward in a straight line, from the starting position to the point of impact. This strike is applied with a thrusting motion, generated by twisting the upper body into the blow. Upon completion, bend your elbow tightly with the fist drawn in near the shoulder. This aids in the contraction of the forearm muscles which must be firm upon contact.

Fig. 7 Do not allow the elbow to swing outward in an arc as it leaves the starting position. This common mistake provides less power behind the strike. The deltoid muscle of the shoulder and pectoral muscle of the chest, when properly employed, generate the energy and strength necessary to carry through the break. The proper contraction of these *Figs. 8, 9* large muscle groups is essential for maximum power in all arm movement.

3: BREAKING: HAND TECHNIQUES · **108**

8

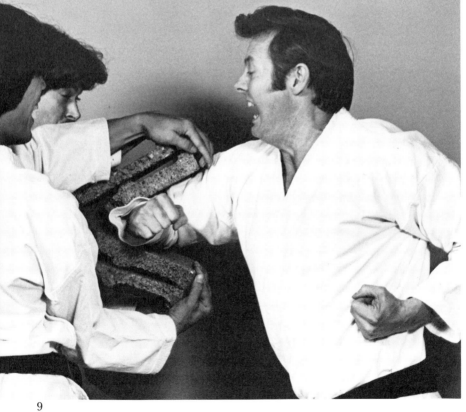

9

10   11   12

Figs. 10–12 VARIATION: A variation of Method 1 brings the elbow into the target in an upward direction. Approximately midway out, the fist begins a 90-degree twist. As previously mentioned, this angle contracts the forearm and triceps muscles which are the areas of contact in the Elbow Strike. To aid in the upward thrust of the arm, twist the upper body in the direction of the target. The hand should be close to the ear, and the elbow should be on a vertical line directly up from the hip upon completion of the technique.

Fig. 13 The properly conditioned student, through a myriad of
Fig. 14 repetitions, should be programmed to complete a move-
(two views) ment. If the arm is halted in its path, coordination between mind and body will be interrupted, ultimately preventing the maximum development of the technique. As the elbow breaks the boards, it must continue upward along its path to the final position.

3: BREAKING: HAND TECHNIQUES • **110**

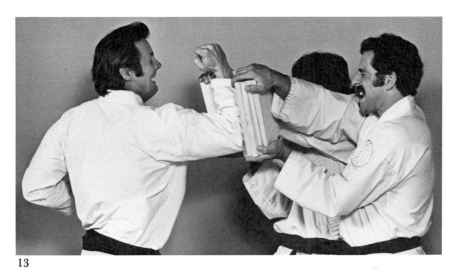

13

14

14'

15   16

Method 2   In Method 2, timing is most important. The body must
Figs. 15–18   be dropped and then tensed in order to focus the elbow
upon contact. Raise your arm high above the shoulder near
the ear. Then bring your elbow down along an imaginary
vertical line to the target. Tremendous speed and power
are generated as the body drops. If the arm deviates from
this straight downward thrust, it may hit the target off-
center. The blocks may then fail to break and injury to the
elbow joint may result.

The greatest difficulty in this method is learning to properly coordinate the drop of the body with the downward
swing of the arm. These two movements must be perfectly
synchronized as impact is made. It is essential, as the arm
starts its swing, that the entire body weight begin to drop
downward. A novice has a natural tendency to lean into
the break, thereby using only the arm and shoulder muscles.
The heavier and stronger muscles in the hip and stomach
region are then bypassed. To avoid this mistake, practice
until both movements are coordinated.

17

18

19   20

19′   20′

Fig. 19   VARIATION: A variation of Method 2, this strike is
(two views)   relatively simple and requires little explanation. The arm
Fig. 20   and elbow must start parallel to the floor, directly in front
(two views)   of the body. The elbow must not deviate from this position
on its way to the target. If it is raised or lowered at any
point along its route, maximum contraction of the chest
and shoulder muscles will not be possible, and strength will
be lost upon contact.

21 22

23

Figs. 21–23   The Double Elbow Strike requires equal development and strength in both arms. However, the popular trend is to favor the stronger areas of the body, thereby neglecting the very areas that would benefit the most from a conditioning and exercise program. Dual development, the application of which is an important aspect of training, regardless of the technique, will take personal stamina and steadfast dedication.

ELBOW STRIKE • **115**

24

Application When used as weapons of defense, each individual area
Figs. 24–30 of the body must be conditioned to counterattack from
every angle.

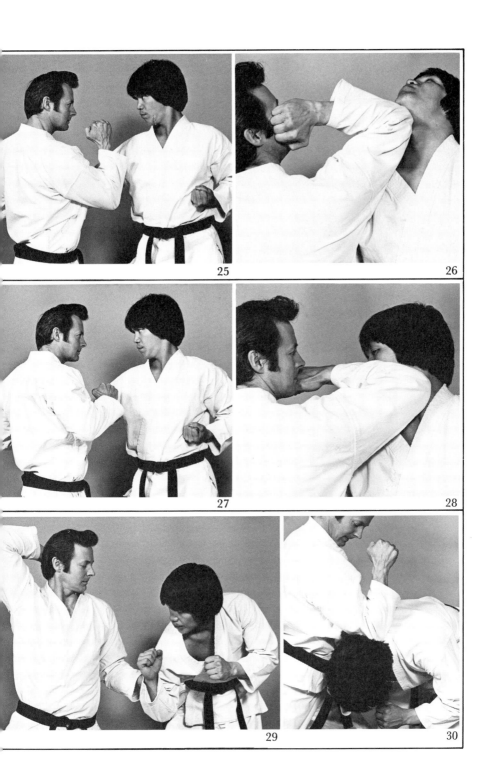

25

26

27

28

29

30

Figs. 31–33   The spinning technique is used when you cannot break
away from an attacker's grip or when you spin away from
an advancing punch. The pivot will bring you to his exposed side.

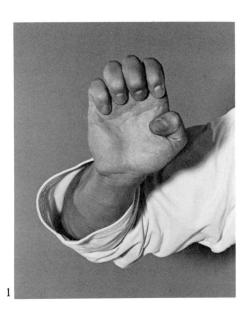

1

■ Palm Heel

Fig. 1

The Palm Heel is undoubtedly one of the strongest hand techniques. By using the heel of the palm as a weapon, you bypass the numerous fragile bones in the back of the hand, palm, and fingers. Contact is made with the strongest and most rigid part of the hand. Held at the correct angle, the palm heel creates a steel-like support from the wrist to the shoulder.

Three basic moves must be simultaneously coordinated to effectively execute the Palm Heel Strike. First, as in most downward strikes, you must drop the body into the target, shifting the body weight from the back stance to the striking arm. Mastering this facet of the technique is essential for effective use of the body weight in the break. Unless this is fully understood, the power generated by the hip and pelvic area will be wasted. Second, upon contact, you must lock the elbow joint to form a solid resistance. Third, you must keep the back perpendicular to the floor while you drop the shoulder slightly to aid in the downward thrust of the movement. Each move in itself is simple to perform. However, to use the moves in a successful, coordinated strike requires much practice.

2   3

Form
Figs. 2–5   To practice the Upward Strike of the palm heel, hold the hand at the hip with the palm face up. Cock your hips in the Back Stance, ready to spring forward. As the hand leaves the hip, twist it to a 90-degree angle. Thrust forward the hip area, adding power to the blow. When the arm reaches full extension, twist your hand an additional 90 degrees. The complete 180-degree twist, from start to finish, creates the crushing ability of this strike. The momentum of the forward thrust, from the action of the rear leg and hip motion, will throw the entire weight of the body behind the impact.

Figs. 6–9   For the Outward Strike, the hand also begins from a cocked position at the hip. Thrust your arm straight forward, keeping it in line with the chest and rib area. In one twisting motion, turn your hand to a 90-degree angle and thrust into the target. When applied properly, this is a devastating attack to the base of the sternum. In this area there is a section of soft cartilage called the xiphoid process. If you break it, your attacker will be disabled immediately by excruciating pain.

3: BREAKING: HAND TECHNIQUES • **120**

4

5

6

7

8

9

10

11

Downward   From the ready stance draw your hand upward. Hold it
Strike   close to your chest with the palm bent inward slightly. As
Figs. 10–13 your hand begins its descent toward the target, shift your
stance forward, transferring body weight to the striking
arm. Finish the follow-through in a low stance, which
positions the hip area below the initial point of contact.
The low stance assures the proper employment of body
weight.

    The shoulder aids in the downward thrust of the arm
upon contact. This is accomplished by shifting body
weight at the moment of impact. Such joint efforts are
what give power techniques their devastating force.

12

13

14

15

15′

Upward Strike
Fig. 14
Fig. 15
(two views)

In this technique, when practiced in an upward position, the breaking material must be held at the same height as the face. Normally, this strike is taught as a technique for attacking the nose or jaw. Therefore, it must be delivered from the correct distance with proper timing. The hips are thrust forward to drive the hand through the target.

16

17

Outward Strike
Figs. 16, 17

For the Outward Strike the material is held at the stomach level. This allows for a strike to the sternum or ribs. A movement's direction affects which muscles react. It is very important that every conceivable direction and angle be utilized, in all techniques, to develop the entire body.

18

22

Application The correct counterstrike to use must be quickly de-
Figs. 18–25 cided as various parts of an attacker become vulnerable.
As your opponent moves, different areas will become
exposed and then disappear. The speed, strength, and
direction of your counter must be evaluated immediately
to select the proper technique for the target.

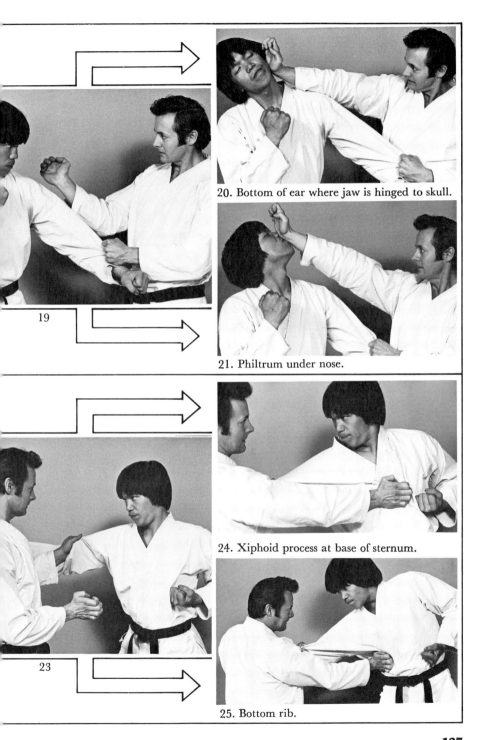

19

20. Bottom of ear where jaw is hinged to skull.

21. Philtrum under nose.

23

24. Xiphoid process at base of sternum.

25. Bottom rib.

1   2   3

■ Hammer Fist

A basic theory of the martial arts is that body energy should be released at the smallest available area. Theoretically, any point of contact made with the body should be no larger than the diameter of a quarter, as demonstrated by the more powerful Side Kick. In contrast, the Hammer Fist is considered strictly a power technique. Because the surface area of the contact hand is larger than a half dollar, the energy released by the body is spread out too far, on impact, to be an effective point of focus. For example, the Knife Hand Strike to the side of the head could cause more damage to the temple than the Hammer Fist directed at the same area.

This technique does, however, serve an important function. The beginner at breaking can use it to feel his power starting to develop. In self-defense, the Hammer Fist is used as a basic and effective blocking technique to the leg, as well as a strong power blow to areas that are protected by heavy bones or thick muscular tissue.

4   5   6   7

Form   Hold your hand at the hip in readiness for the striking
Figs. 1–3   movement. When you decide on the point of impact—in
              this case, the head area—begin to swing your arm in a full
              circle. Bring it behind your back and over your shoulder in
              the way you would wield a sledge hammer. As your hand
              comes over your shoulder, you should have your arm fully
              extended with the elbow slightly bent. At the moment of
              contact, drop the entire weight of your body into the
              downward thrust. You do this by simultaneously lowering
              the stance and bending the knees.

Figs. 4–7   VARIATION: A variation of the Hammer Fist Strike moves
              to the rib area. As your hand starts toward the target, it
              begins an outward arc from the hip. For maximum chest
              and shoulder muscle contraction, you must keep your arm
              on the same parallel plane throughout the movement. If
              you raise or lower your arm while it is moving, different
              muscles will be alternately tensed and relaxed, lessening the
              effect of the blow.

8   9   10

Strike All movements require concentration. In power techniques such as the Hammer Fist, accuracy is also extremely important. One of the primary objectives of concentration is to focus the mind on the point of contact. If a strike is delivered off-center and the material does not break, the hand and arm will absorb the entire force of the blow. The elbow should remain bent throughout the technique to minimize the shock at the elbow joint.

Figs. 8–12 The Hammer Fist makes contact with the bottom of the fist, with the entire body weight behind the swing of the arm. The shoulder muscles, which contribute enormously to the power of this technique, must be developed in both size and strength. Twist the upper body in the direction of the strike in order to completely utilize shoulder and arm thrust.

11

12

13   14

Hammer   When properly used, this block makes contact with the
Fist Block   foot at its weakest point. As the kick is rising, the fist blocks
Figs. 13–15   the side or top of the instep bone. The pressure created on
impact, from the foot coming up and the fist going down,
can easily cause the instep bone to shatter.

Figs. 16, 17   To develop power which will lead to confidence, practice
the break shown in Figure 16 at the same angle you would
apply the block. Once contact is made and the bone
broken, the fist follows through in order to push the leg to
the side of your body.

15

16

17

18

Application
Figs. 18–22
The forward thrust of the hip and stomach area must be slightly ahead of the moving arm. Targets on the body that require a strong forceful blow are the top of the head, side of the neck, chest, and rib cage. Like the sledge on the end of a swinging hammer, the speed and power of the hand are controlled by the arm.

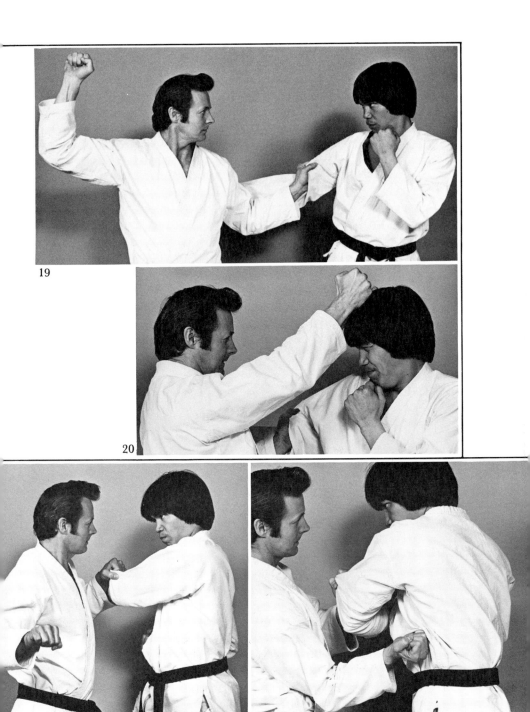

19

20

21

22

■ Spear Hand

The Spear Hand is probably one of the most difficult and painful breaks to execute. Hundreds of nerve endings in each finger require years to condition, along with many diligent, time-consuming exercises to strengthen the small, weak muscles which control the fingers. Because of this technique's difficulty, it is rarely seen. When viewed, however, it commands immediate respect.

There is no easy way to perfect the technique, but I have listed a program for those of you who want to try. If you follow it, success should come in little time. However, you should note that this move is never done without difficulty or pain.

Even though the Spear Hand is associated with all five fingers, only three (the index, middle, and ring finger) actually make contact. Conditioning should be concentrated on them. Strengthening the finger tips is the first goal. The exercises for finger-tip push-ups listed on page 138 must be followed religiously. They are essential in building the finger muscles. Calluses must also be formed on the finger tips to lessen the pain caused by tender nerve endings. To do this, constant and numerous hand thrusts into a pail of sand are mandatory.

To prevent your nails from splitting, keep them well trimmed and cut square across, continually clipping along the edge to thicken the nail. After conditioning with the sand pail, clean under the nails to avoid infection.

When the fingers have been developed to your satisfaction, it is then time to attempt an actual break. For the first break, the board should be 3 inches across, the approximate width of the three contact finger tips. After a few practice breaks, you will be able to judge the exact angle to hold your fingers and whether your nails have been cut short enough. You will then be ready to graduate to a board with a 4-inch width. This width should still be relatively easy, depending on your size and strength, but some pain at this time is not unusual. More conditioning may be needed along with the mental conditioning necessary to accept pain. At this point, you should acquire the respect due this technique.

Advancement is now made to a 6-inch board. Serious students can usually reach this point; however, progress to

1   2   3   4

the 8-inch regulation tournament boards (for this particular technique) appears to be an obstacle for most. It is at this point of resistance that many abandon the break. To pursue the break beyond this obstacle usually involves many additional months of dedicated practice. For those who reach the 8-inch goal, satisfaction and respect will be gained from mastering a very difficult technique.

Form
Figs. 1–4
The Spear Hand Strike is executed in the same way as the Forefist Punch. The hand starts its move from the hip with the palm up. As it leaves the hip, it begins a twisting motion at the wrist. Hold the fingers firmly together with the thumb curled inward. As the striking hand moves forward, draw the opposite hand to the hip with equal speed. At the same moment that the arm of the Spear Hand reaches its full extension, the retracting hand reaches the hip.

5   6

Practice
Figs. 5, 6

Condition the fingers by repeatedly thrusting the hand into a pail of sand. Align the fingers as shown to ensure equal development of the three finger tips. The container for the sand must be deep enough to drive the hand in at least up to the knuckles. This allows all the finger joints to meet resistance, thus building their strength.

Figs. 7–9

Your hands will also benefit from variations of three-finger push-ups, which require hundreds of repetitions to increase finger strength. They must be practiced daily.

Pointers
Fig. 10

A common mistake made with the Spear Hand is to hold the fingers straight out with the joints locked. If the joints are locked upon impact, the fingers will tend to push up-ward. The middle finger will absorb the entire shock of the blow, which may dislocate it.

Figs. 11, 12

The correct way to hold the fingers is at a slight angle inward. The middle finger is drawn in so that the three finger tips make contact together. It is essential to tense the muscles of the hand simultaneously as impact is made. This will prevent the fingers from collapsing inward upon contact. The tension on the hand is evident in Figure 12 as the fingers penetrate through three 6-inch-width boards.

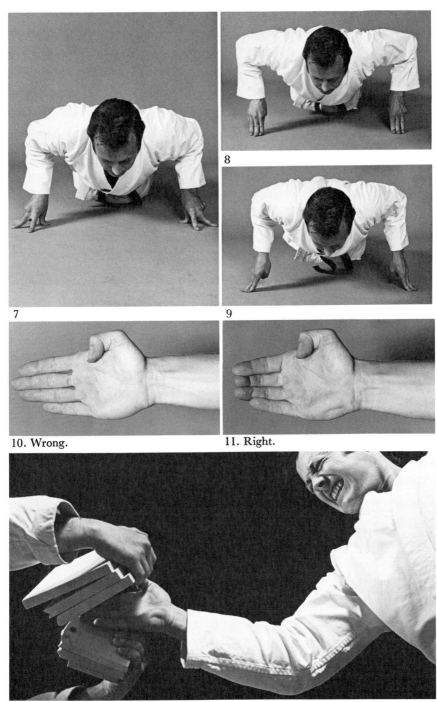

7

8

9

10. Wrong.

11. Right.

12

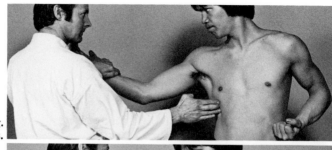

13. Wrong.
Sternum and ribs.

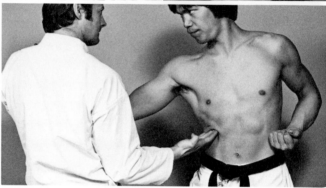

14. Right.
Under bottom rib.

Application   As mentioned elsewhere in this text, always apply your breaking techniques to self-defense. In the case of the Spear Hand, familiarity with the human anatomy is necessary to use the technique effectively. A common mistake, shown in books and taught in schools, is to attack the wrong areas of the body. If you are going to use a counterattack effectively, you must be aware of the body's vulnerable areas for that particular technique. Since the Spear Hand has limited power as a striking movement, the areas on a human target where it can be applied are also limited.

Fig. 13   The sternum and rib area can be compressed up to 2 inches under a pressure of 80 to 120 pounds without causing fractures. Therefore, to attack the ribs with a Spear Hand is useless. Although there is a space between the rib bones that is vulnerable, the thickness of cartilage, muscle, and clothing prevents the fingers from penetrating the area. The average student probably weighs in the neighborhood of 130 to 170 pounds and, unless he is a true master of this technique, his penetrating capacity will be limited.

Fig. 14   Do not attack an area without knowing your objective. The correct area to attack is under the bottom rib. Vital organs, located in this general area, are vulnerable targets.

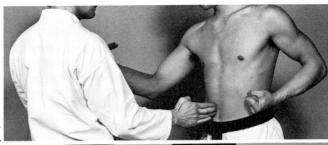

15. Wrong.
Stomach.

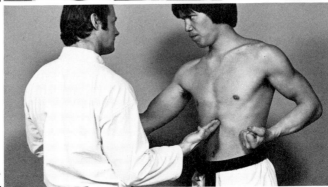

16. Right.
Solar plexus.

The liver is located high up on the right side along with the gallbladder, which is attached to the underside of the liver. The pancreas, although less prone, lies behind the stomach on the left side. Located on either side of the spine, at the level of the lowest ribs, are the kidneys. Sufficient pressure to any of these sensitive areas will immediately cause nausea and will nullify any further attack.

Fig. 15   Another mistake commonly made with the Spear Hand is to attack the stomach. The majority of men, in fairly good shape, can take a well-delivered blow to the stomach. It would seem obvious, then, that a Spear Hand to this area is useless. The only injury would probably be the rupture of blood vessels around the thick muscles protecting this area. This, however, would not stop an advancing attacker bent on causing you bodily harm.

Fig. 16   The correct area to focus your blow on is the solar plexus. The solar plexus is a nerve center at the pit of the stomach that has no muscular protection. It is an area, approximately the size of a half dollar, located just below the sternum bone of the chest. Any Spear Hand attack to the solar plexus or lower rib area must be directed upward to penetrate to the inner organs.

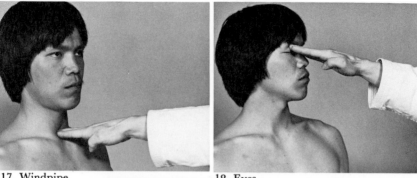

17. Windpipe. 18. Eyes.

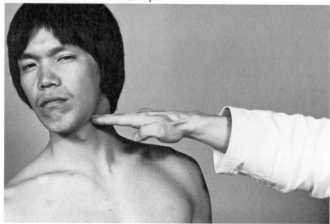

19. Carotid Artery.

Figs. 17–19   The Spear Hand can be used against such other vital and sensitive areas as the windpipe, eyes, and carotid artery.

■ Ridge Hand

The Ridge Hand, because of its limited power, is seldom used. Nevertheless, it is still an important technique to be developed by all martial arts students. It is a particularly effective blow to the vital areas of an attacker. To condition the side of the hand used as the ridge, use either a *makiwara* board or a heavy bag.

1   2   3   4

The accompanying illustrations show how the hand is hooked into the target for breaking, and also how it can be used as a weapon for defense. When working against an opponent, remember to bring the Ridge Hand over his front hand and hook it into his body. Be sure to maintain this same angle when lining yourself up to the breaking target. Never practice a breaking technique differently from the way you would practice it for fighting. As a rule, breaking and fighting practice should not conflict, but should be used to complement each other.

Form
Figs. 1–4

The Ridge Hand makes contact with the inner edge of the forefinger knuckle. Pull in your thumb as far as possible to avoid making contact. As your hand leaves your hip, it travels in a slight horizontal arc. Do not allow your arm to enter a roundhouse swing. As it begins its arc from the hip, it is then hooked into the area of impact. Angle your hand downward as contact is made.

Figs. 5–8   VARIATION: A variation of the Ridge Hand starts from the hip as above. It then begins a full circular swing over the shoulder and behind the body to gain momentum. Hip motion is important in this technique. You must thrust your hip forward to give the arm a whipping effect upon contact. In any technique that has limited power, speed becomes the key factor. To increase the speed of a movement, hip action and arm swing must be coordinated. As the handle action of a whip controls the speed of its tip, the hip action of the body controls the speed of the arm.

9

10

11

Inward Strike:
Palm Down
Figs. 9, 10

Hold the striking hand at the hip with the palm up. As it is snapped toward the target, it arcs outward from the hip. When the arm approaches the target, twist your wrist so that the hand will thrust through the board with the palm down.

Speed Strike
Fig. 11

Because the target is hanging free, the ends of the board will meet no resistance. Therefore, the strike will be accomplished with speed rather than a thrusting movement. If the speed generated is great enough, it often will cause both ends to fly away from the assistant.

12

13

14

| **Outward Strike: Palm Up** *Fig. 12* | This variation starts with the hand at the opposite hip, palm down. The arm arcs slightly outward as it travels across the chest. As the arm approaches the target, the hand twists at the wrist, and the strike makes contact with the palm up. |
| **Upward Strike: To Groin** *Fig. 13* | The Ridge Hand is used effectively as a strike to the groin in self-defense; therefore, it should also be practiced at the groin level when breaking boards. This is necessary to give the student the perspective required to judge the proper angle, direction, and height of the strike. |

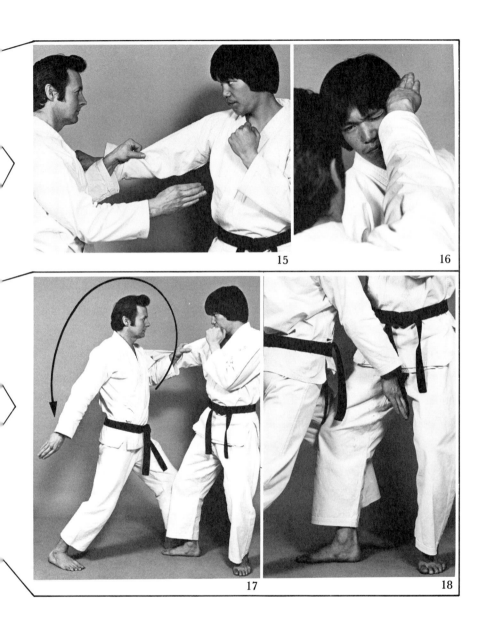

15   16

17   18

Application
Figs. 14–18

When you use the Ridge Hand as a weapon of defense, you must attain sufficient arm swing to gain maximum speed and momentum. As in any technique, full muscular contraction is made upon contact to increase the force of impact. Vital areas of the body that can be effectively attacked with the Ridge Hand are the temple, throat, nose, and groin.

■ Back Fist

The Back Fist makes contact with the rear of the knuckle on the forefinger and middle finger. Bend your wrist to deflect the blow from the back of the hand on impact. The blow is delivered with a downward snapping motion of the arm. The elbow must remain bent throughout the movement, especially when contact is made. If the elbow is locked, the joint will be snapped upward (the elbow's weakest position) causing possible injury and leaving you vulnerable to counterattack.

The strike of the arm, for breaking purposes, must be coordinated with the forward thrust of the body. This synchronized movement emanates a force that can easily break two boards or fracture the nose of an attacker.

The technique can also be used to keep an opponent off-guard or to measure the distance for a follow-up punch. The martial arts student uses his front hand in a Back Fist Strike much as the boxer uses his front hand in a jab.

Form
Figs. 1–4
(two views)

This technique is performed using the front arm in a quick snapping motion. Bring the striking hand alongside of the opposite ear. Shift the front leg back about 12 inches (depending upon your own height). As your hand starts toward its objective, it begins a slight downward arc. Return your front leg to its original position, causing the weight of the body to shift from the back leg to the front leg. This forward momentum of the body, coordinated with a sharp snap at the wrist, creates the speed and focus for the blow. Do not use the back of your hand to make contact. When you complete the strike, twist your fist downward so that only the knuckles hit the target. The elbow must not travel beyond the side of the body. Since the elbow controls the whipping effect of the hand, it must be aligned to the fist and target at all times. Do not allow the upper body to lean into the strike. This would offset the center of balance, which should be on a perpendicular line, centered between both legs.

Front view.　1　　　　　　2　　　　　　3　　　　　　4

Side view.　1'　　　　　　2'　　　　　　3'　　　　　　4'

5   6

7

Straight   Begin in a Back Stance with the right foot facing the
Back Fist target. Shift your right foot back approximately 12 inches
Figs. 5–7 while you draw your punching hand up to the opposite
ear. Then thrust your entire body forward, snapping your
punching hand into the center of the target. Do not push
your fist through the break, but quickly withdraw it as
soon as the boards are broken.

The technique as shown here is applied from the Back
Stance, but any of the strong attacking stances can be
used. The important thing to remember, however, is not to
allow the stance to rise as you move toward the target. The
center of gravity must remain on an equal plane, from the
start to the finish of the movement, for maximum power.

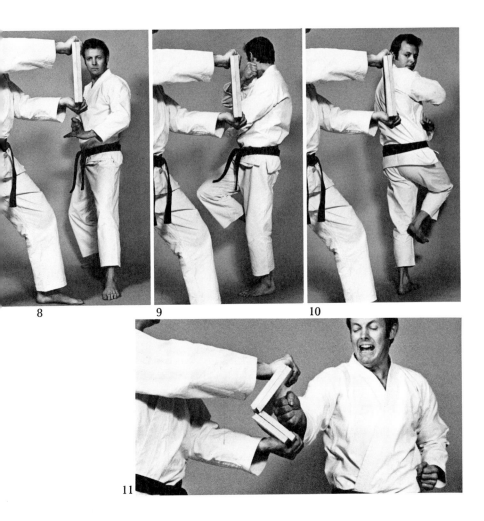

8 9 10

11

Spinning Begin in the same stance you used for the Straight Back
Back Fist Fist, except that the opposite (left) foot should face the
Figs. 8–11 target. As you start the pivot, draw your rear (right) foot
up to the left knee with the attacking hand approaching the
opposite ear. As you finish the pivot, have the attacking
hand at the ear ready to be snapped into the target. The
right leg (now the front leg) is ready to be dropped into its
proper stance as you thrust your body forward to aid the
momentum of the moving arm. The boards are held for
this technique at an angle different from that for the
Straight Back Fist. Due to the spinning of the body, the
arm will be carried outward to complete the circle, thereby
causing it to approach the boards from the side.

12

Application
Figs. 12–16
Use this strike to attack the vital areas with a sharp snapping movement. It is delivered in a downward direction, with a slight angle to the side.

Areas to strike include the temple, nose, and cheekbone. Due to the small target area and moving head of the attacker, accuracy is extremely important.

If the attacker has grabbed your front arm, use the spin to bring the rear hand into position for a strike to his exposed side.

13

14

15

16

■ Speed Break

The Speed Break or Suspended Break is a technique used to measure the speed and snap of your punch. This break is usually practiced with one or two boards; emphasis is placed on increasing the snap of the fist into the target.

When you work on a technique, it should always be complemented by a Speed Break variation. In this way, the speed of a movement can be developed as well as power and penetration. Speed Breaks are usually done in one of the following ways: either by dropping the target in the air, or by hanging the target from a string. The Speed Break can be applied to almost every striking movement taught in the martial arts.

Strike
Fig. 1
Hold the boards at about arm's length. The shoulder and arm of the punching hand must be relaxed and ready to spring forward.

Fig. 2
When the distance to the target is measured and the proper level of concentration is reached, drop the boards.

Fig. 3
The forward strike of the hand must be timed perfectly in order for the knuckles to make contact with the exact center of the boards. If impact is made above or below the center, the boards will not break. Because the shoulder remains relaxed throughout the movement, it will be thrust forward into the break. However, the upper body must remain straight so as not to interrupt the speed generated by the twisting of the hips.

Figs. 4, 5
In order to execute Suspended Breaks, it is essential to develop the speed required to accelerate the point of impact past the surrounding area. The inertia at the ends of the board will remain slightly behind the contact point, and the board will bend until it breaks. When a blow does not generate the necessary speed, the entire board moves as one mass and the board flies away from the force without breaking. There are limitations to the force a board can withstand before breaking. Therefore, because the board has a fixed mass, only the acceleration of the contact area, caused by the blow, can provide the force necessary to break the board.

6

Variation
Fig. 6   The most difficult variation of Suspended Breaks is to place a long narrow board between two pieces of paper. To set up this break you will need two pieces of paper cut approximately 10 inches wide by 18 inches long, a long narrow piece of wood 1 inch thick, two swords, and two assistants.

Insert one of the swords into one of the pieces of paper approximately 6 inches from the top and midway between the sides; do the same with the other sword and paper. With two assistants now holding a sword each, make a cut in the paper approximately 6 inches from the bottom through which you can insert both ends of the wood. Some initial tearing can be expected from the weight of the wood.

The speed of the strike must be capable of breaking the board before the ends are pushed downward, tearing through the paper. The degree of difficulty can be increased by varying the thickness of the paper, the thinner paper being the more difficult.

1

■ Thumb Strike

Though this break is a rarely seen technique, it has been included in this book because it receives high marks in tournaments when executed successfully.

The ligaments, tendons, and muscles must be developed to their maximum to absorb the entire shock of the blow, or the thumb will break. Because of the angle the thumb is held at, the knuckle joint cannot absorb any of the blow.

Fig. 1   Thumb push-ups are the best exercise to strengthen this part of the hand.

2

3

Fig. 2   This technique can be developed in the same way as the
Spear Hand. Use a narrow board to begin with and then
gradually increase its width.

Application   The nerve at the corner of the jaw hinge affords the best
Fig. 3   opportunity for the Thumb Strike as a counterstrike
against an opponent.

4

Breaking:
Kicking Techniques

■ Front Kick

Figs. 1–3
(p. 162)

From the Back Stance, bring your rear leg forward and up. As you raise your rear foot, it must remain on a straight line to the target. Bring it up quickly from the floor to the knee of the stationary leg. This assures that the groin will be protected from a surprise counterattack. From this position, the knee of the kicking leg is instantly aimed at the target. Remember, the foot cannot kick higher than the knee once the knee has become locked. Therefore, if you bring your knee up too low to the target, your foot will not reach its point of impact on center. If the knee is brought up beyond the center of the target, the foot will follow suit and hit above center.

A common mistake in correcting errors made in height is to raise or lower the leg at the hip after the knee has been locked. Since the hip is important for the power in this technique, any movement interrupting this forward thrust will obviously reduce the power of the kick.

1   2   3

4

Application The Front Kick is used against the primary vital areas
Fig. 4 of the body. They run along an imaginary line from the
face to the groin. This includes the neck, heart, solar
plexus, and abdomen.

5

6

7

8

Strike

Figs. 5–8

A strong stance is as essential as the proper distance from the target. There are two important things to keep in mind when breaking with the front foot: Know at what angle the boards are held to meet the rising foot, and be sure the ball of the foot is the only area to make contact.

Breaking with the Front Kick is usually accomplished using a thrust movement. A thrust movement continues through the broken material, since the knee is held locked. To get maximum power, twist the hip in a forward motion. At the same time that you thrust the hip forward, move the ball of the foot into contact with the target, and lock the knee.

9   10

Figs. 9, 10   Probably the most important phase of the thrust is the forward movement of the hips. Figures 9 and 10 show how and when the hip is thrust into the kick. Figure 9 shows the line the hips should be on as the leg moves toward the target. Figure 10 shows the distance the hip is thrust forward as the foot makes contact, approximately 4 inches. The hip thrust must be practiced to coordinate with leg extension.

■ Front Instep Kick

Figs. 1, 2   From the Back Stance, bring the kicking foot forward and up to the knee of the opposite leg. Point the toes down so
Fig. 3   that they do not make contact. From this position, the leg
(two views)   travels to its point of impact in a sweeping upward motion. Bend the upper body slightly forward to maintain a strong balance and to thrust the entire weight of the body behind the kicking leg.

1

2

3

3′

As in all kicking techniques, once the leg is fully extended and contact made, snap the foot back to its original position. This recoil action should be an instantaneous reflex to prevent the opponent from grabbing your leg.

FRONT INSTEP KICK · **165**

4

Application
Fig. 4

The Front Instep Kick is applied in the same manner as the conventional Front Kick, except that it is directed to the groin. The leg thrusts upward in a sweeping motion between the opponent's legs.

Strike
Figs. 5–8

Snap the kick from the floor to the target in a sweeping upward motion. A second assistant is necessary to prevent broken pieces of boards from flying upward.

This type of kick is seldom used for breaking because of the fragile unprotected nature of the instep bone. Because contact with the boards will be painful, take several practice shots before the actual break. This is to ensure that the toes are completely curled out of the way and the thicker part of the instep bone is in alignment for the break. The toes must be curled downward to avoid their making contact. You must also hold the ankle in an extended position to prevent the foot from making contact off-center.

4: BREAKING: KICKING TECHNIQUES • **166**

5

6

7

8

To demonstrate the effectiveness of this kick to the groin, the boards should be held at approximately the same angle for the line of direction that the instep will be traveling.

1   2

■ Roundhouse Kick

Figs. 1, 2   The stance for the Roundhouse Kick is basically the same as that for the Front Kick. The similarity ends when the rear foot is brought up to the height of the opposite knee. As the rear foot reaches the opposite knee, begin to pivot on the ball of the foot of the supporting leg. At this point balance is important, since all your weight will be on the stationary leg. Continue to raise the kicking leg until the ankle and knee are parallel to the floor. You then start the kick itself by snapping the foot from its cocked position.

Fig. 3   The snapping motion at the knee and the swinging of the
(two views)   hips must be simultaneous. Move the foot in a circular motion to strike an imaginary line in front of your body. The foot angles downward as it snaps into the desired point of impact. Curl the toes tightly inward to avoid contact. Immediately after the leg has reached full extension, snap the kicking foot back into its cocked position, and then lower it to the floor.

3

3'

4

Application
Fig. 4   The Roundhouse Kick is used against the secondary vital areas of the body. They run along an imaginary line from the temple to the ankle and include the ears, sides of the neck, ribs, and knee joints.

5

6

7

Strike	Place the target so that the kick will focus directly in

Strike
Fig. 5   Place the target so that the kick will focus directly in front of the body. Alignment must be exact, so that the ball of the foot hits the target dead center.

Fig. 6   As the kicking leg begins to rise, the hips start to pivot toward the target. Twist them to bring the kicking foot into range. Lean the upper body into the direction of the kick to add additional thrust behind the leg.

Fig. 7   From the cocked position, thrust the kicking leg into the target. Whip the foot outward, extending the leg until the knee becomes locked. After breaking the material, recoil the foot back to its cocked position, then lower it to the floor.

1   2

■ Standing Side Kick

Fig. 1   Start the Standing Side Kick from the same stance as the previous kicks. However, as with the Roundhouse Kick, pivot on the stationary foot as the kicking leg reaches the knee. The amount of power generated will depend upon how well you use your hips. To ensure maximum power, you must not pivot your hips beyond the center of the target, nor should you stop them before the center of the target. The pivot must stop as the hips line up with the dead center of the breaking material. From the starting position to the cocked position, the stationary foot pivots

Fig. 2   90 degrees on the ball of the foot.

3

Fig. 3   From the cocked position, thrust your leg into the target. The next movement, which is easily overlooked, makes the Side Kick the powerful weapon that it is. As you make contact with the target, pivot the stationary foot an additional 90 degrees. This causes the entire weight of the body, especially the hip area, to move toward the target. The momentum of the body thrusting forward an additional few inches means the difference between breaking two boards and breaking four. If you do not have a strong Side Kick, I recommend this additional 90-degree pivot.

Figs. 4, 5   The strength of the Side Kick is greatest when the upper torso is on a vertical line with the stationary leg. If you lean back as far as 45 degrees you will reduce your strength. Beyond 45 degrees the strength of the kick will dissipate more rapidly until it becomes completely ineffective.

Various styles in the martial arts utilize different sides of the kicking foot. Some use the blade edge, others use the heel. Both adaptations serve a purpose. However, for breaking, you should use the stronger bones of the foot. In

Fig. 6   the case of the Side Kick, the heel represents the strongest and least fragile area to make contact with a solid object. The toes of the foot must be pointing downward. This position (of the toes) adds strength to the kick because the twisting of the foot causes the muscles of the kicking leg to contract. As muscles are contracted, energy is produced, thereby increasing strength.

4. Right. 5. Wrong.

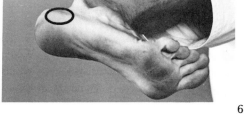

6

7

Application   The Side Kick is effective in strikes to any area of the
Fig. 7   body.

1   2

■ Walking Side Kick

Figs. 1–4   This variation of the Side Kick can be employed from
the Back Stance. However, it is more often executed from
the Side Stance (both feet facing the front with the body
weight centered between the legs). The Side Stance, sometimes referred to as the Horse Stance (*kimase* in Korean,
kiba-dachi in Japanese), is indigenous to all styles of the
martial arts. As you move toward the target, shift the rear
foot to a spot just beyond the front leg. As the body weight
shifts to the leg that has been brought forward, draw up
the opposite leg and cock it at the knee. When the full
weight of the body is balanced upon the stationary leg,
thrust the cocked leg forward. As contact is made, the knee
of the stationary leg is locked and the heel planted with as
much force as possible into the floor. A 90-degree pivot on
the ball of the stationary leg is also required. This moves
the hips forward and generates power into the heel of the
kicking foot.

3   4

5

Application
Fig. 5
The Walking Side Kick is used to make up a short distance between you and your opponent. Although a point of contact may have been chosen, to initiate the move, the kicking leg can be directed to any area of the body once it has become cocked.

WALKING SIDE KICK · **175**

6   7

Shifting the rear foot.

Strike
Figs. 6, 7   You must correctly judge the distance between you and your target prior to executing the move. You can only do this by numerous repetitions of the same move, bringing the back foot to the front, and shifting the body weight forward.

Fig. 8   As you shift the weight of the body forward and balance on the supporting leg, draw the kicking leg upward and cock it at the knee. At this point you can instantly calculate the distance to and height of the target, to assure a coordinated thrust into the material.

Fig. 9   At the exact moment of impact, pivot the stationary leg 90 degrees on the ball of the foot. This pivot will move the body in the direction of the kick, increasing the kick's force, momentum, and thrust.

8

9

1   2

■ Hopping Side Kick

Figs. 1–4   The most powerful version of the Side Kick is executed with a hopping movement into the target. This variation is also employed from either a Back Stance or Side Stance. You must thrust the entire body forward with a hop in the direction of the kick. This is done by moving the rear foot forward to replace the front foot. Both feet will leave the ground. While off the floor, draw up the kicking leg and cock it at the knee. As your rear foot touches the floor (moving forward to where the front foot was), thrust the cocked leg into the target. Use the same 90-degree pivot, on the ball of the stationary foot, used with previous Side Kicks.

Application   The Hopping Side Kick can be utilized against any area
Fig. 5   of an attacking opponent. The final 90-degree pivot adds a significant input of power over the Standing and Walking Side Kicks by moving the body forward only a few inches. The coordination of this pivot with the momentum of the body moving forward three or more feet is devastating.

3

4

5

6. Back Stance.　　　　7. Side Stance.　　　　8. Hopping forward.

Strike
Figs. 6–10
The greatest focus will be exerted with the kicking leg on a straight line out from the hip. The higher the foot is brought above the hip joint, the weaker the kick will become. When breaking with the Side Kick, keep it low. Do not sacrifice strength for height.

Do not lift the heel of the supporting leg off the floor. The stronger the support of the stationary leg, the stronger the kick. The strength in a stance is generated downward from the hip to the heel, not to the toes.

9. Breaking five 1-inch boards.

10. Breaking one 4-inch cinder block.

1   2

■ Front Hook Kick

Figs. 1–4   From the Back Stance, bring the front foot back and up
to the knee of the opposite leg. The kicking leg begins to
rise at a 45-degree angle to the front of the body. Raise the
foot to a position just above the intended point of focus. As
the leg reaches full extension, hook it in, at the knee,
toward the contact point. Draw the foot into the target at
a slight downward angle. Then allow it to continue on its
path back to the starting position. This uninterrupted circular motion allows the momentum of the body, created
by the twist at the hips, to add speed and power to the
technique.

Application   The Front Hook Kick, when used against an opponent,
Fig. 5   is brought up to the rear of his front shoulder. It is then
hooked behind his front arm into the side of the head, neck,
or face.

4: BREAKING: KICKING TECHNIQUES • **182**

3

4

5

6   7

Strike
Figs. 6, 7

This technique utilizes the front leg in an upward hooking motion. As the kicking leg (front foot) leaves the ground, bring it from the floor to the target in a semicircular motion.

Figs. 8, 9

Bring the leg to full extension with the foot higher than the target. When the leg reaches the proper height in relation to the target, draw the foot into the target in a snapping motion from the knee.

For maximum strength in this kick you should start the foot in a downward path before making contact with the material to be broken. After breaking the target, the foot must continue without interruption to complete the circle. This will bring the kicking leg back to its starting position.

4: BREAKING: KICKING TECHNIQUES • **184**

1

■ Back Hook Kick

Figs. 1–4   From the Back Stance, once aligned with the intended point of contact, you start to pivot on the ball of the front foot. Spin backward approximately 90 degrees until the contact point is sighted. In all martial arts techniques, the eyes should not leave the target or opponent any longer than necessary. In this case, for the 90-degree pivot, the eyes leave the point of contact for a split second. Spinning techniques require the head to turn faster than the body. The upper torso follows and then the hips, causing a whipping effect of the legs into the target. As you sight the target, begin to raise your kicking leg in the same circular motion used for the Front Hook Kick. Then hook the leg into the point of impact. The foot travels without pause; it must continue in a downward path to its starting position to fully utilize the momentum of the spinning body.

Application   The Back Hook Kick utilizes an unexpected change of
Fig. 5   direction to secure an advantage over an opponent. The backward spin creates the illusion that you are moving away from his advance. In fact, this elusive move allows deeper penetration into his defenses. It is carried off by drawing his forward movement into your perimeter of defense, and then striking from a different angle.

6   7

Strike Gauging the proper distance to the target is extremely
Figs. 6–9 important. Your heel must make contact with the center of
the boards.

As you sight the target, after you pivot to the rear, begin
to raise your kicking leg to its cocked position. As the foot
leaves the floor, it does not pause in its path until it is re-
turned to the starting position. Bring the leg to full extension with the foot higher than the target.

The momentum of the spinning body will give a whipping effect to the kicking foot. As the heel penetrates the
target, it must continue back to its starting position without
interrupting the momentum gained.

BACK HOOK KICK • **189**

1   2

■ Back Thrust Kick

Figs. 1–3   From the Back Stance, as your head turns to line up the
target, bring your kicking foot up to the knee of the supporting leg. From this cocked position, thrust it straight
back into its objective. The "straight back" in this movement cannot be overemphasized. Although most kicks get
weaker as the leg goes higher than the hip, in the Back Kick
strength dissipates even more quickly from the slightest
elevation above hip level. The strength from the hips cannot
be generated in an upward direction with the leg extended
to the rear of the body. To compensate for this loss, it is
necessary to capitalize on the large percentage of strength
generated in this technique by the muscular contraction of
the leg muscles. To accomplish this, hold your foot with the
Fig. 4   heel extending farther than the toes. The toes must face
downward and curl toward the knee. This angle of the foot
causes the muscles from the back of the thigh to the bottom
of the calf to contract, adding increased strength to the
movement.

3

4

5

Application
Fig. 5

The Back Thrust Kick is utilized as a defensive maneuver to the rear of the body. It is effective as a power technique to areas of the body from the solar plexus to the knees, which include the ribs, abdominal area, hip joints, and groin.

6

7

8

Strike
Figs. 6–8

Have the target in sight, out of the corner of your eye, before executing the kick.

First, bring the foot of the kicking leg up to the knee of the opposite leg. At this point, cock the foot in order to begin to thrust it into the target. As you uncoil the leg toward the target, twist the upper torso in the direction of the kick. Thrust the kicking leg straight back to its objective, extending the hip, until the knee is locked.

4: BREAKING: KICKING TECHNIQUES • **192**

1. Stance.

2. Upward angle.

3. Outside angle.

■ Knee Break

Figs. 1–3 From the Back Stance thrust the knee straight up and forward, or in an arc at a slight outside angle. When using the knee in either angle, the direction of focus is changed. Therefore, it should be practiced both ways. This will ensure confidence no matter what angle you are attacked from.

5   6

Figs. 4, 5   Practice breaking with the knee from both directions. This will strengthen the muscles of the leg at both angles.

Application   The knee is used as a weapon whenever an attacker has
Fig. 6   penetrated your perimeter of defense. If he has made, or is about to make, contact, use your knee. Depending upon the location of the attacker, the knee can be thrust into his ribs, solar plexus, or groin.

4: BREAKING: KICKING TECHNIQUES · **194**

Advanced Breaking

1

■ Combination Breaking

An often overlooked method of practice is the use of different kicking techniques in combination. Some techniques require speed, while others require strength or agility, and their development in combination can only add to your skill as a martial arts student. Practicing double or triple techniques in breaking not only forces the body to develop the spinning and twisting movements in coordination, it also allows the student to develop focus and contact with accuracy.

Front Kick and Back Kick
Fig. 1

Each of these kicks, executed alone, is not difficult. However, in combination, difficulty arises from trying to focus with the same leg moving in two different directions. Figure 1 shows your position in relation to the assistants holding the boards.

2

3

4

Fig. 2   For the first kick in combination, either use a front snap or front thrust. Do not allow the foot to travel through the break. When you break with combinations, the leg should not pause after contact with the first target. If the leg travels through the broken material, there may be a delay in the recoiling of the foot for the second break.

Fig. 3   Bring the kick immediately back to the cocked position as you turn your head to see the next target. As the leg begins its backward path, you must twist your foot to point the toes forward and extend the heel outward.

Fig. 4   The speed of the leg and the thrust of the hips must be timed as they move toward the target. Coordinating this

5

6

7

8

movement is essential; if it is not synchronized as contact is made, the body will be pushed forward, off-balance, thereby diminishing the power of the movement.

Roundhouse Kick and Front Hook Kick *Figs. 5–8* Begin by throwing the Roundhouse Kick with a very rapid snapping movement. Break the first target with a sharp, speedy motion, then instantly pull the foot straight backward. The foot must travel in a straight line to hit the second target in the center.

Snap the heel through the boards. Then hook it back to a cocked position at the knee, and lower it to the floor.

COMBINATION BREAKING · **199**

Roundhouse Kick and Back Hook Kick
Figs. 9, 10

Figure 9 shows your stance in relation to the persons holding the boards. The first kick in this combination is the Roundhouse with the left foot. Although the Roundhouse Kick itself is relatively simple, it is most important to place your left leg properly as you bring it back to the ground. You will have to practice this to find the suitable kicking height and length of stance. You must replace your left foot in a position that will allow the body to begin its turn into

Fig. 11 the Back Hook Kick. As this foot touches the floor, begin to raise the right leg.

Fig. 12 As with the Back Hook, you must sight the target prior to starting the kick. Bring the foot to a position slightly higher than the center of the second target, and then hook it downward into the center of the boards. As the foot travels through the break, it continues in a downward path back to a cocked position and then to the floor.

13

14

15

Figs. 13–15   Use this combination against an attack from opponents. Notice that the leg for the Hook Kick is brought above the attacker's arm and shoulder, and then hooked downward into the side of the head, face, or neck. Combination breaking must be practiced in order to build confidence in using multiple attacks against one or more opponents.

16   17

18

Jumping Double Front Kick
Figs. 16–18

This technique is usually executed from a normal standing position facing the target. The body must remain completely relaxed to ensure maximum height. As you spring upward, draw the knees up toward the chest. When you attain maximum height, snap the left foot into one of the targets.

19

Fig. 19   As the body continues to rise, snap the opposite foot into the remaining target. The purpose of practicing this technique is to develop focus, not once but twice, while both feet are off the ground. The speed developed to execute this break will prove useful when you work on less demanding techniques.

Jumping Front Kick and Jumping Roundhouse Kick
Figs. 20–22

In this combination, both of the breaks are accomplished while the body is off the ground.

The Jumping Front Kick is executed with the left foot, as the body travels upward. While still traveling upward, the body must begin its turn toward the second target. The hips will twist from the upward momentum of the second kicking leg. The targets can be held at different heights and angles to increase dexterity.

20

21

22

Knee Break and Side Kick
Figs. 23–25

Use the knee in an inside Roundhouse motion that would attack the bottom rib rather than the solar plexus. After you break with the knee, hold it in the cocked position while you turn your head to line up the second target.

As the kicking leg starts toward the target, bend the knee

Fig. 26   of the stationary leg slightly. This allows maximum focus when the knee is again snapped into a locked position while the kicking foot makes contact with the target. As contact is made for the Side Kick, use the 90-degree pivot, which has been fully explained on pages 171–72. This cannot be overemphasized.

27   28

29

Figs. 27–29   Use the knee whenever an attacker has penetrated your defense and has, or is about to, make contact with you. At this angle the knee can break a rib, thereby disabling the first attacker. The Side Kick is then used to halt the forward momentum of an advancing second attacker. In this case, the foot thrusts into the side of the chest cavity, damaging or breaking the ribs, and incapacitating the second attacker.

■ Brick Breaking

Breaking bricks is a very difficult art. Although I do not guarantee that everyone can perform this break, for not all can, I do feel there are many with this capability. It must be remembered, however, that a break of this caliber requires years of dedication and hard work. It will not materialize overnight, nor, for that matter, from one year to the next. Students, often misled by articles written on the ease of breaking bricks, become discouraged by their failures. Don't give up too soon. Most of these articles are written by advanced black belts with 20-odd years of experience. Is it any wonder you don't find the break as simple as they do?

Of the more difficult techniques, brick breaking is also the most publicized. Its popularity is due in part to the availability of bricks and their easily recognizable characteristics of strength and durability. Because of these properties, the difficulty of the break is universally accepted and respected. Even advanced black belts place those who have mastered this break on a pedestal. It is no wonder that students are fascinated by it.

To succeed in brick breaking, you must be completely confident of your ability and properly condition your hands to sustain the force of the blow. Dedication toward a specific goal is essential in this break more than in any other. This section will help you in acquiring the mental attitude necessary, along with a comprehensive program of methods designed to help you achieve your goal. The program consists of three separate methods of brick breaking, Method 1 being the easiest. Even though only the Knife Hand is illustrated here, the Hammer Fist, Palm Heel, and Reverse Punch can all be used to accomplish this break.

The Hammer Fist, the least difficult of the above techniques, should be practiced first using Method 1, Method 2, and then Method 3. You can then continue on to the Palm Heel, Reverse Punch, and Knife Hand, keeping them in this sequence and making sure to apply each to all three methods. All three methods can be practiced by a beginner without fear of injury, provided that the four types of strikes listed have been perfected.

The purpose of Method 1, the simplest of the three, is to condition the mind. This is very important, for the mind must be thoroughly convinced that the brick will break. Without this confidence, although your body is physically capable, your mind will set up barriers that will make the feat impossible. Even this simpler method will give you a feeling of power as the brick breaks. This initial feeling is the foundation on which true confidence can be built.

Method 1
Figs. 1–3

A solid platform is essential. A concrete block turned on its side is sufficient. The platform should be approximately stomach-level to utilize fully the power in the hip and pelvic area. Place a piece of carpet or a folded handkerchief under the left hand. Balance the brick in the left hand so that the opposite end is about 1 inch off the surface. Reverse hands if you are left-handed. The timing in this method is the most important factor. The breaking hand must make contact with the center of the brick at the exact moment the free-hanging end hits the solid surface.

Using this method will accomplish two things. It will perfect your timing, and it will increase your self-confidence by overcoming any psychological obstacles to brick breaking.

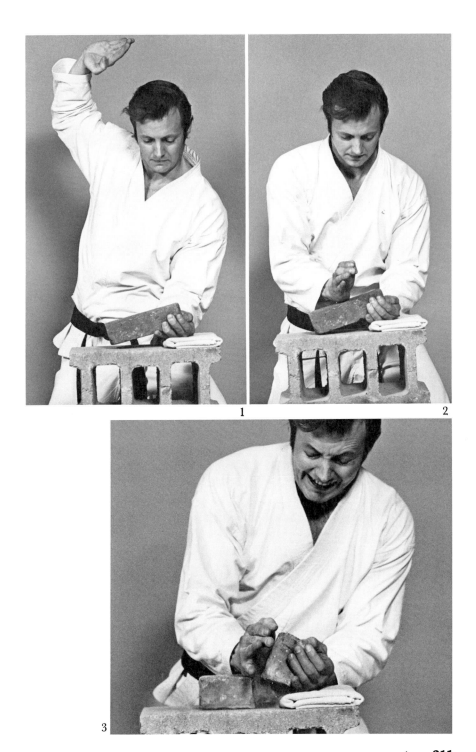

1

2

3

4   5

Method 2   For support, place a brick under each end of the brick
Fig. 4   that is to be broken. A handkerchief or other piece of
material can be placed on the center of the brick. This will
cushion the blow and prevent the skin from being cut. Line
up the hand to the point of contact; be sure the angle of
the strike is correct. Rest your left hand on the supporting
brick on the left side. Using your thumb, index, and middle
fingers, raise that end of the brick approximately 1 inch off
the surface.

Figs. 5, 6   As the breaking hand makes contact with the center of
the brick, simultaneously drop the raised end. The amount
of speed and force with which the raised end is driven down
onto the support brick will determine the ease of the break.
Before delivering a full-force blow, practice timing the
striking of the brick while dropping the raised end until they
are coordinated.

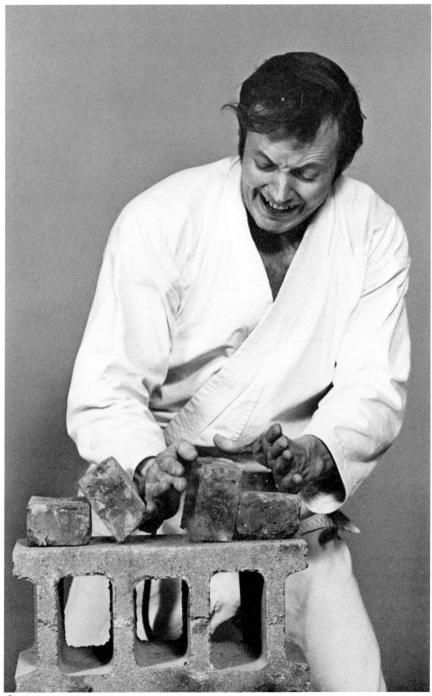

6

7   8

Method 3
Fig. 7
Full mental concentration is essential before the strike. The mind must be free of distractions. You must know, upon contact, that the brick is going to break. If you have not achieved this confidence, you are not ready for Method 3. If you doubt yourself at all, you will unconsciously hesitate at the moment of impact. This will cause the force of the blow to spread across the surface of the brick, and the only thing that may break is your hand.

It requires approximately 140 pounds of pressure to break a brick. To get this degree of force in your Knife Hand Strike, you must have the proper mental attitude. You must have mastered the angle of the Knife Hand and conditioned the heel of the palm to protect the wrist. This method should not be attempted until the other methods have been completed.

Figs. 8, 9   As your hand strikes the surface, you must have complete control over all your body movements. Your hand must make full contact and be allowed to follow through. The entire muscular system is tensed, especially the stomach, hip, and pelvic area. As mentioned previously, this is a difficult break. Once achieved, it is worthy of respect.

■ Breaking with the Head

All breaking techniques carry an element of risk, but few are as potentially dangerous as breaking with the head. For this reason, it is ill-advised to continually indulge in this technique, even though the head can be successfully and effectively used as a weapon of defense. For the student intent on this break, however, a full understanding of its hazards and the proper angling of the head upon impact are imperative. It should be remembered, and I cannot stress this enough, that when the head is thrust with speed and power into an immovable solid object, it starts in motion a series of events that can lead to self-inflicted harm.

An immediate medical problem which may occur is a concussion. This is caused by severely jarring the brain. A concussion of the brain is actually a paralysis of its function. Symptoms of concussion appear immediately, but vary depending on the degree of injury. They include severe aching of the head, a weak dizzy feeling, and visual disturbance. Whenever a concussion is suspected, consult a physician at once. An X-ray examination should be made to determine whether or not a fracture of the skull or other complications have occurred.

The continuous pounding of the skull is never recommended, nor is it necessary. A condition, commonly referred to as being "punch-drunk," is caused by the scar tissue formed by continually abusing the sensitive tissue of the brain. Depending on the areas affected and the degree of damage, this condition could result in slurred speech, loss of vision, or diminished reflex action.

In a typical breaking technique, the head is thrust toward a target, the brain remaining slightly behind the forward momentum of the skull. As impact is made, the brain accelerates to the speed of the movement and slams into the wall of the now stationary skull. When the head retracts from the point of impact, the brain is thrust backward to make contact with the opposite wall of the skull. Thus, in a single thrust, the brain has been exposed to two serious jarring movements. Consequently, there is a momentary wave of very high pressure inside the skull which is transmitted to the brain. This is believed to cause many small hemorrhages, creating pressure often responsible for headaches, unconsciousness, or death.

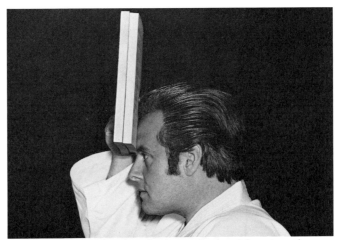

1. Wrong. A break using the lower forehead is extremely dangerous and should never be attempted.

2. Right.

Fig. 1   Extreme care must be taken to avoid making contact with the lower forehead. Located slightly to the sides and above the eyebrows are the hollow sinus cavities. If the head hits the target with the flat section of the forehead just above the eyes, the thin-walled sinus cavities may collapse inward. And if the lower forehead is fractured, bone fragments of the front wall may be driven through the back of the thin-walled sinus cavity and into the brain.

Fig. 2   To prevent such injuries, the correct angle of the head to the target utilizes only the upper forehead as the area of contact.

Figs. 3, 4   To start breaking with the head, and to minimize jarring the brain, it is recommended that the boards be held firmly by hand and drawn into the pre-selected area on the upper forehead. This method allows the break to take place without fear of injury from hitting the target off-center by using a forward thrust into the boards. The most common mistake made with this method, however, is to overcompensate for the angle and make contact with the top of the head.

5

Variation
Fig. 5

The most often-used variation of this break is also the most unsafe. This method uses blocks or boards placed on stationary supports. This is dangerous because the target will not give way if the initial impact fails to break the objects. In addition, the downward thrust of the head is at a critical angle. In an unconscious effort to drop the weight of the body into the break, a student may make contact with the flat of his forehead, including the section containing the hollow cavities above the eyes. Any one of these crucial factors can cause the injuries previously described.

Breaking:
Flying Techniques

Flying techniques are usually used for demonstration purposes. They should be practiced and perfected nevertheless, to increase dexterity and maneuverability. These techniques are useful when running toward a target. They provide the leverage needed to reach a distant object by allowing you to leave the ground and travel through the air. The timing required for breaking, while the body is traveling horizontally off the ground, encompasses a new area of development. This phase of breaking techniques requires you to lift, turn, cock, and focus the body, all the while moving through the air.

The flying techniques are shown through the use of consecutive drawings. The different positions of the legs, as the body lifts off the ground until it reaches the target, can best be shown by drawings in sequence, rather than numerous photographs.

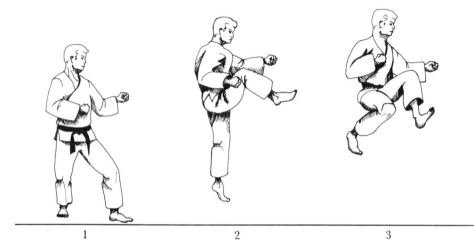

1　　　　　　　　　　　2　　　　　　　　　　3

■ Flying Side Kick

The most familiar of the flying techniques is the Flying Side Kick. This must be mastered as a prerequisite to the other flying techniques. Its importance is stressed because it incorporates all of the necessary movements that make up the flying kicks. The jump, twist of the body, cock of the legs, and focusing while traveling in a forward direction, when perfected, will make development of the other flying techniques easier to understand and accomplish.

Figs. 1, 2   Figure 1 shows the stance as you reach the spot chosen to start the jump. The leg used to spring off the ground will become the kicking leg. You must pull the opposite leg upward and cock it at the knee. The higher this knee is drawn upward, the higher a strong spring off the kicking leg will take you. The coordination of these two initial movements is essential for maximum height and forward momentum.

4   5   6

Figs. 3, 4   Pull the leg used to spring off the floor upward and in toward the body. At this point, your body has reached its greatest height. Cock the bottom leg close to the body and begin to align the upper leg with the target. It is important to bring both knees as high as possible to obtain maximum height.

Fig. 5   Start the kicking leg out toward the target. Hold it in this position (approximately midway out) until it is within the proper striking range.

Fig. 6   Now, thrust the kicking leg forward and lock it at the knee. The bottom leg must descend rapidly to the floor to support your body as you drop through the broken material. It is important to remember that in most of the flying techniques, the upper body must remain inclined, at a slight angle from the vertical, in the direction of the kick. If the upper body is inclined at any other angle, away from the direction of the kick, you will slow down your forward momentum and lessen the effectiveness of the kick.

■ Flying Front Kick

The Flying Front Kick utilizes its height and momentum in a vertical rather than horizontal direction. Therefore, if good height is desired in this technique, the program of leg strengthening exercises beginning on page 30 must be followed. A rule of thumb to remember, to help judge your jumping height, is to gauge your kick by the height you can achieve above your own head. In other words, if you can jump straight up to a height of 7 or 8 feet, then you can also kick and break an object at that height.

Fig. 1   Figure 1 shows the stance as you reach the spot chosen to start the lift-off. Place the foot that will spring the body upward on this spot, and walk backward to the point where you will start your approach. The number of steps required will have to be determined individually; however, you must practice the number of steps decided upon for the approach to assure proper timing and distance for lift-off.

1 2 3

4 5 6

Fig. 2   Begin to push off the kicking leg, while you draw up the opposite leg close to the body and as high as possible.

Figs. 3, 4   Now pull up the kicking leg by cocking it at the knee. The higher you raise this knee in the direction of the target, the greater the height you will achieve. Bring the kicking leg up from the floor to the cocked position, and then start it toward the target without any hesitation. The upward momentum, caused by the pulling action of the kicking leg, draws the body to its maximum height. As you draw within striking distance, keep the kicking leg on the same path and snap it into the target.

Figs. 5, 6   Quickly withdraw the kicking leg to a position that will support a landing in a strong balanced stance. The final movement of any technique must be prepared like any other move in that technique.

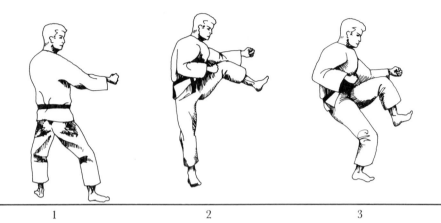

<table>
<tr><td>1</td><td>2</td><td>3</td></tr>
</table>

■ Flying Roundhouse Kick

The Flying Roundhouse Kick utilizes its momentum in the same vertical direction as the Flying Front Kick. The major difference between the two techniques is the pivot of the hips while in the air. This twisting motion of the hip and pelvic area is necessary to bring the kicking leg into the target from an outside angle. Any change of direction while traveling vertically interferes with the upward momentum of the body and can lower the maximum height you would like to obtain. Therefore, to minimize this effect, you must make the pivot quickly and smoothly.

Fig. 1   As in any breaking technique, your eyes must focus on the center of the target from the moment you begin to move in that direction.

Figs. 2, 3   Begin to push the kicking leg while you draw up the opposite leg close to the body and as high as possible. Now pull up the kicking leg in a continuous swing from the floor to the cocked position.

Fig. 4   At this point, twist the hips with a rapid snapping motion. The pivot of the hip area adds to the momentum of the kicking leg and brings it into the target in an outside swing.

Figs. 5, 6   As you draw within striking distance, allow the kicking leg to continue its momentum into the target. Quickly withdraw the kicking leg to a position that will support a landing in a strong balanced stance.

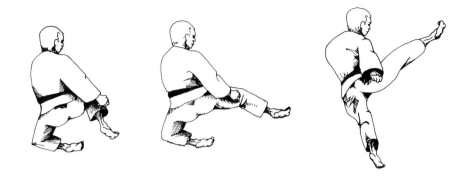

4   5   6

1   2

■ Flying Back Kick

The Flying Back Kick, like the Side Kick, utilizes the momentum in a horizontal direction. This horizontal movement is the only similarity, however, between the two kicks. Before attempting this technique while traveling over an object or person, practice first with a simple one-step and jump. Face the target, jump straight up and spin in the air, and then thrust out the leg for the break. This one-step move will develop the main points of the break before you progress to more advanced movements.

Figs. 1–3   As you leave the floor, quickly tuck the kicking leg upward and close to the body. Start immediately to turn the head and the rest of the body in the air.

Fig. 4   Your body is now traveling backward toward the target. Turn your head slightly to one side so that you can see the target out of the corner of your eye. Cock the kicking leg so that it is ready to thrust out into the target. Hold up the opposite leg more or less, depending on the height of the objects you are jumping over.

Fig. 5   As the kicking leg is thrust through the material, you must drop the opposite leg down to support your body as it reaches the ground.

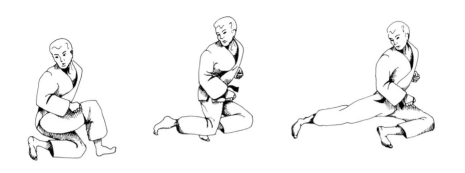

3   4   5

Method 1.

1

■ Flying Double Front Kick

The purpose of this technique is to use the ball of each foot simultaneously to break an object. There are two methods to start your push-off from the ground. One is the conventional broad jump where both feet spring off the ground at the same time. The other method is the normal one-leg push-off that is used in most of the flying techniques.

Method 1
Figs. 1, 2

After you determine the initial distance from the beginning to the end of the approach path, plant both feet simultaneously on the spot previously chosen for push-off. To make sure you travel far enough in the air, synchronize your lift-off. Place both feet on the point of push-off while bending both knees as in a running broad jump; then spring up and out toward the target.

Fig. 3

Draw up both knees close to your chest. At this point, the body is at its greatest height. Now release your legs from the cocked position. As they start toward the target, bend your body slightly forward to increase momentum and power.

Fig. 4

As contact is made, thrust your legs straight out until your knees become locked. Then quickly lower your feet in order to prepare for landing.

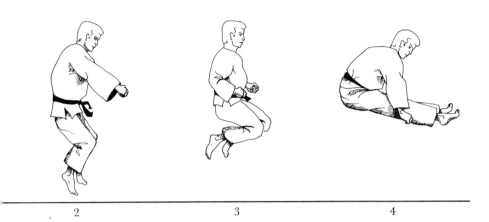

| 2 | 3 | 4 |

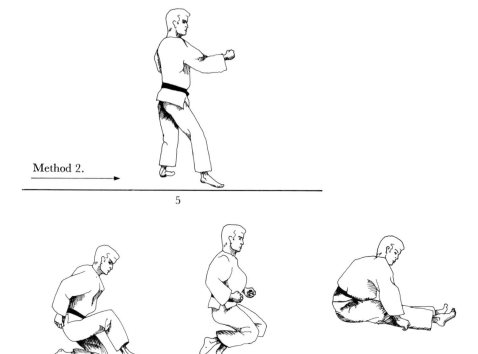

Method 2.

5

6   7   8

Method 2   As you reach the spot chosen for push-off, you can use
Fig. 5   either leg for the push-off. Draw your other leg upward
with the knee bent. This upward pull of the non-kicking leg
will aid in the momentum of the push-off. At push-off,
Figs. 6, 7   draw up your kicking leg until the knee is bent. At this
point, both knees are tucked and the body should be at its
greatest height.
Fig. 8   Now release your legs from the cocked position. As they
start toward the target, bend your body forward slightly to
increase momentum and power. As contact is made, thrust
your legs straight out until your knees become locked. Then
quickly lower your feet in order to prepare for landing.

Demonstration Breaks

■ Samurai Melon Cut

Many breaking techniques have inherent risks. Serious injury is an ever-present possibility, especially in the more spectacular breaks performed for demonstrations. Advancement in any of these techniques is not instantaneous, but should be attempted gradually as progress is made in the art. A program must be followed through various stages of difficulty. Concentration, repetition of movement, and self-control, which involve untold hours of practice, are the primary ingredients necessary for perfection.

Partners are used in many of these techniques. It is unfortunate that they must be used, for the very fact they are there indicates the hazardous conditions involved. It is an additional responsibility to consider the danger to anyone participating in the demonstration. Before jeopardizing another person, make a careful evaluation of your discipline, confidence, and mental ability. No absolute guarantee can be given for another's safety; however, in your mind, no doubt should exist that you have mastered the technique. It cannot be overemphasized that you should not exceed your capabilities. Take note that many of these more difficult techniques are reserved for black belts. The years of study necessary to attain this degree, leave little time in the workout program to practice demonstration techniques. The black belt is the beginning. The foundation is now set for developing inner abilities to complement external accomplishments.

Method
Figs. 1, 2
(p. 238)

Line the sword up to the target at a point that brings the blade horizontal to the floor (approximately the navel).

Raise the sword high and back; then swing downward until the blade is horizontal to the floor. To keep the blade on this level plane throughout the cut, bend your knees, thereby lowering the entire body and sword through the cut.

Fig. 3

The upper body must not lean forward. It remains straight and drops into the cut. This is accomplished by coordinating bending the knees with lowering the body. At the exact moment you cut through the melon, the sword must be drawn upward to avoid contact with the assistant's body.

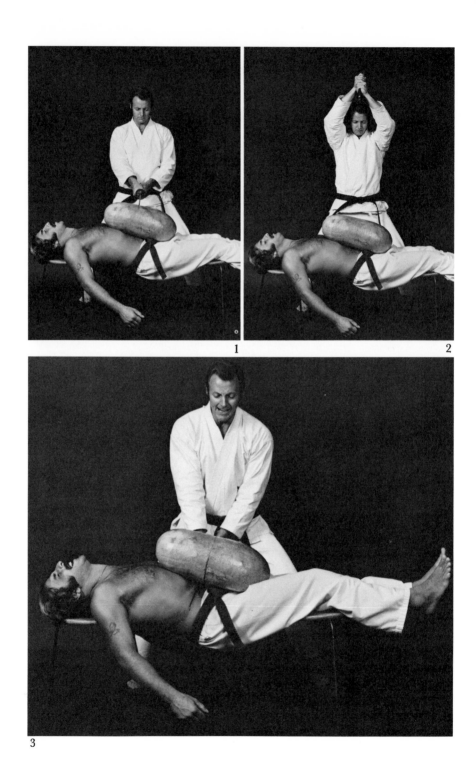

1

2

3

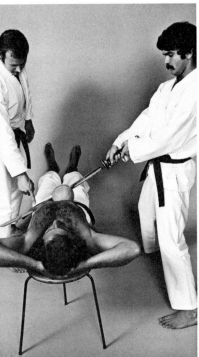

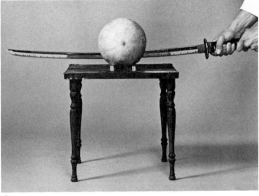

5

6

4. Wrong.

Pointers

Fig. 4   If you allow the upper body to lean forward on the downward swing, the sword will enter the cut on an angle. This will cause the blade to catch the side of the assistant's stomach before severing the fruit.

Fig. 5   To measure the progress made in controlling the sword, place the melon on a bench. Put an object, such as a wooden matchstick, under the fruit. When the fruit can be severed without cutting the matchstick, you can then start to use an assistant.

Fig. 6   When using an assistant in practice, use a sword with a dull edge. Allow the assistant to leave his uniform top on and, if he prefers, place something the thickness of a magazine over the uniform where the fruit will be cut.

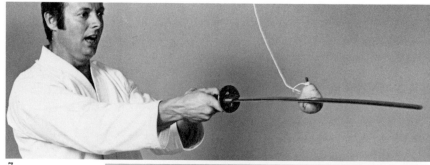

7

8

Fig. 7   To develop the ability to halt the momentum of the moving blade, tie a soft fruit, such as a pear, to a string. Then swing a samurai sword at great speed into the fruit, the objective being to cut without complete penetration. This will be difficult in the beginning, as the momentum created by the tip of the sword will cause the blade to continue on its path through the fruit. You will find that swinging a samurai sword hundreds of times is no easy matter. The entire arm, from the wrist to the shoulder, will become sore until these areas are developed to handle the movement.

Fig. 8   Two swords should be used for this technique: one with a dull-edged blade for practice, and one with a razor-sharp edge for actual demonstration. Objects of various sizes are used in practice. The smaller the object, the harder it will be to halt the sword in its path. Fruits and vegetables that may be used are pears, watermelons, honeydews, cantaloupes, and cucumbers.

■ Bed of Nails

The Bed of Nails was only introduced in this country within the last few years. It is used strictly for demonstration purposes, as it holds no other practical use to the martial art student. The mental benefits derived from developing this technique can of course be applied to other areas of training. I can only appease skeptics by demonstrating that this is not the magic of some ancient Oriental priesthood. Nor does it involve faking.

For the student who wishes to master this technique, there are some serious obstacles to overcome. The primary one is the pain responses transmitted by the brain. These pain impulses can be interrupted to a large degree through the use of self-hypnosis. This does not mean that you have to be in a semiconscious state, but rather that by auto-suggestion you can increase your resistance to pain. The depth of your achievement will depend largely on your mental attitude and grasp of self-hypnosis.

To put it in athletic terminology, the more you psych yourself up, the less pain you will feel. In the same way, an injured football player can complete a game without feeling pain or a tournament fighter can finish a match without feeling swelling or bruises. To some extent psych and self-hypnosis are one and the same, as they both achieve the same results.

Another problem which may present itself is the danger of being cut by one of the nails. The cut is usually a puncture wound, which by itself would be no cause for alarm. However, this type of wound can easily be contaminated by tetanus bacteria, especially if the nails are rusty. A tetanus infection can be fatal, as it causes spasmodic rigidity of the voluntary muscles, particularly those of the lower jaw. Do not minimize the danger involved. Get a tetanus injection before attempting this technique, and contact a doctor in case of any injury.

1

2

Method
Figs. 1, 2   In this technique, the assistant uses a sledgehammer to break a stack of blocks resting on your stomach while you lie on the bed of nails. The assistant lines up the hammer to its point of contact and then raises it straight up and back. As it descends, it must fall at a precise angle and with great force.

Fig. 3   At the moment of impact, you must tense all the muscles of the entire body. This spreads out the pressure caused by the hammer pushing through the blocks. Needless to say, the stomach muscles must be well-developed, since they absorb the major shock of the blow.

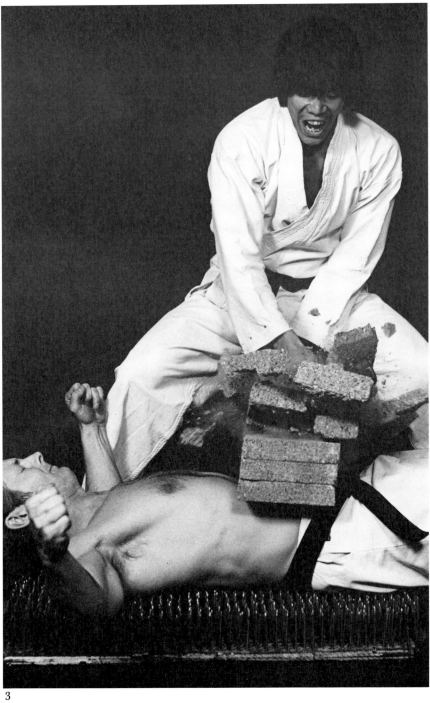

3

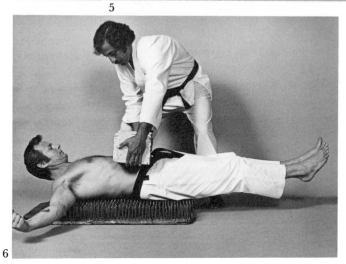

Pointers	To make a bed of nails, you need a sheet of one-half inch plywood, approximately 22 inches wide by 30 inches long, and about 500 sixteen-penny nails. The nails are placed one-half to one full inch apart in consecutive rows.
Fig. 4	To lower yourself on the nails, sit on the edge and use your arms to let yourself down. The first few times you attempt this, do not allow your full weight to rest on the nails.
Fig. 5	As you allow more pressure to rest on the nails, lift your feet off the floor and bring your arms out to the sides to balance your body.
Fig. 6	Once you can remain on the nails for about 30 or more seconds, have an assistant place a cement block across your stomach. This will add additional pressure from the nails against the skin of the back.

7: DEMONSTRATION BREAKS · **244**

■ Bottle Cut

The Bottle Cut, although first introduced in this country over a decade ago, has, until recently, rarely been attempted. Its difficulty goes without question. However, prompted by public support of the various martial art demonstrations touring the country, and the demand for more spectacular exhibitions, many of the top-ranking black belts have mastered this technique. Much of the upsurge in new techniques, and the reappearance of old ones, is due to the highly commercialized aspects of an expanding market in the martial arts. The Bottle Cut in the future should enjoy a popular revival.

It cannot be overemphasized that this technique should not be tried by the inexperienced student, nor even by a black belt unschooled in breaking. Most demonstration techniques are difficult and involve some degree of danger. The Bottle Cut is a technique as dangerous as it is difficult. I doubt if anyone can attempt time after time to knock the top off a bottle without at one time or another getting seriously cut. Of the thousands of martial arts practitioners across the country, probably only a handful have successfully performed this break. It must be realized, from the beginning, that even after dedicated practice, success is not always achieved. This technique, however, deserves your highest esteem.

Much of the difficulty experienced in executing it lies in the horizontal direction that the arm must travel, as opposed to the more conventional downward swing. At this angle, the point of contact on the edge of the hand will be more sensitive than normal, due to the position of the pisiform bone. In the downward strike, as explained in the section on the Knife Hand (p. 93), the pisiform bone lies behind and beneath the meaty section of the palm heel. However, at the horizontal angle, this sensitive bone has less protection and is therefore more vulnerable to injury.

Generally, the horizontal swing is weaker than the downward swing of the Knife Hand. Body weight cannot be fully utilized in a strike across the front of the body. Therefore, 90 percent of the strength of this attack depends on the speed of the hand. In addition to the tremendous speed that must be generated by the arm for this technique, an equally important facet is mental attitude. The mind must

1

2

3

be calm and completely empty. Only with the mind under control and united with the physical energy being generated, will the bottle break. If at any time, from the initiation of the arm movement to contact with the bottle, you are conscious of surrounding diversions, the technique will not work. The slightest interruption, lack of confidence, or fear of injury will prevent the mind and body from blending in concentration toward this goal.

Method   A whiskey bottle or any similar long-necked bottle is preferable for this technique. In order to keep the bottle stable while the top is being broken off, fill the bottle no more than half-full with water or sand.

Figs. 1–3   Bring your hand back and high to fully utilize the strength of the upper body as it twists into the strike. Practice rotating your hips while you simultaneously swing your arm on either a *makiwara* board or heavy bag until your timing on impact is accurate and precise. You must develop

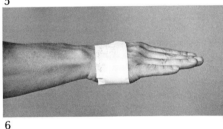

4

5

6

the side of your hand until it is firm and callused. This provides solid resistance as the surface of the hand meets the surface of the bottle. As you make contact, the entire muscular system of the body is tensed and then instantly relaxed. The ability to do this is a key to this technique.

Pointers
Fig. 4   The hand must be conditioned to prepare for the Bottle Cut. Muscles in the shoulder, chest, and forearm have to be strengthened through continuous repetition at the same angle as the strike.

Fig. 5   Accurate positioning is also extremely important. Although the bottle will move from the path of the hand, if contact is made on the fifth metacarpal knuckle, the speed of the strike itself may shatter this fragile bone.

Fig. 6   During practice, the back of the hand can be covered with adhesive tape. This will prevent the hand from being seriously cut, if it has a tendency to drop into the strike rather than traveling straight through it. Remember, as the top breaks away, the back of the hand will be only a hair's distance above the razor-sharp edges of glass on the remaining bottle.

■ Fire Breaks

In most demonstration techniques, showmanship with a flair for the dramatic will go over well with an audience. Exhibition techniques are limited and audiences have probably seen them all. They are there to be entertained and, after they see bricks and blocks broken time and again, attendance may dwindle. To add new interest, initiative is essential, as many standard techniques can be imaginatively transformed to prevent boredom. The majority of spectators do not realize the difficulty in breaking a brick; in fact, they assume it is easy. Because of this attitude, demonstration programs must be kept fast-moving with innovative new ideas.

The Flying Side Kick, as an example, has probably been seen so often, by so many people, that it is now rarely even done for demonstrations. Nonetheless, it is a beautiful movement when executed properly. You need only to add some imagination, and you have renewed interest for both the audience and yourself.

It must be pointed out that unless you are an experienced practitioner of the art, these demonstration techniques should not be tried. The movements by themselves are not difficult, but when you add nails, fire, or glass you are greatly increasing the degree of danger. These techniques should not be toyed with by the inexperienced or attempted without supervision.

Flaming Hoop
Fig. 1

The hoop must be sturdy enough to permit accidental contact with the sides. Ordinary lighter fluid is used to ignite the hoop. Do not use gasoline, which does not burn itself out almost immediately like lighter fluid. The hoop illustrated here has a $3\frac{1}{2}$-foot diameter; sizes vary and should be made to fit the individual.

Fig. 2

A comfortable hoop allows the body to go through without sacrificing style by crouching. A poor entrance into the hoop, as demonstrated in Figure 2, can cause the rear foot or shoulder to make contact with the edge, thereby breaking the jumper's concentration.

Fig. 3

The body must be fully tucked prior to entering the hoop. This allows total concentration on the target as the body travels forward. The fire should be eliminated during practice to prevent distraction. Once mastery is attained

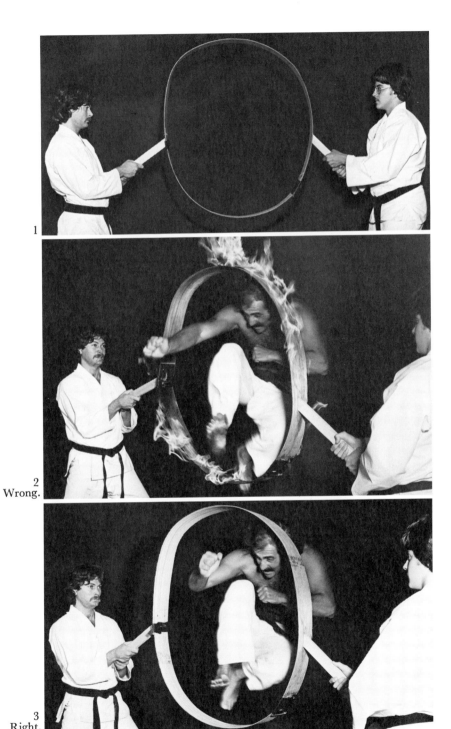

1

2
Wrong.

3
Right.

4

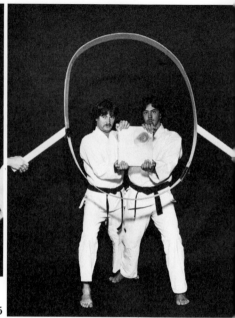

5

over the movement, flames can be added. You can control the intensity of the fire by varying the amount of combustible liquid.

Fig. 4   This technique must be performed with the uniform top removed. Caution must always be used when working with fire. Remember, the hair on your head is vulnerable and burns easily, and the cloth used for the uniform is flammable. As a precaution, when working on this technique, have a wet towel on hand to extinguish any accidental spillage of the liquid. Also keep in mind that most carpets and floor waxes are flammable. If control of the hoop is lost and it's dropped on a carpet or waxed floor, you may have trouble explaining what happened to the local fire department. If at all possible, practice this technique outside until it is perfected.

Fig. 5   When looking through the hoop, even with the flames, the assistants and boards will always be visible. Your first concern should be a well-executed kick as you enter the hoop. Once your body goes through, your eyes can then focus on the center of the target. Do not sacrifice control of your technique by worrying about the target prior to getting through the hoop.

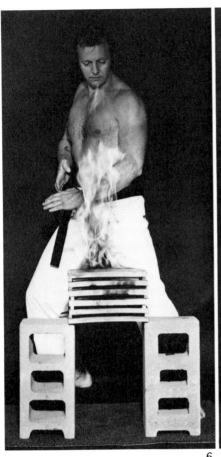 

6   7

**Flaming
Board Break**
Figs. 6, 7

The Flaming Board Break utilizes 1-inch boards placed on top of each other with half-inch spaces between them. The spaces increase the effect of the flames, which will engulf the boards from the bottom to the top, as the hand follows through.

Lighter fluid is used as the combustible element. It is placed on the bottom and top boards. The liquid on the bottom board is ignited first. To be sure the flames will climb the outside of the middle boards, some of the liquid may be placed along the edges of each board. The flame from the liquid itself will not rise that high (approximately 12 inches) but, as the striking hand travels through the boards, oxygen is drawn into the flames, increasing their height to upward of 3 feet.

8

Figs. 8, 9   In this technique, clothing or skin may catch on fire. The uniform top should be removed because of its flammability. After completing the break, be sure to check that the lighter fluid is not burning on your skin. In most instances, you do not feel any pain until the skin has already burned a few seconds. As a precaution you should always be aware that the boards will be flying in all directions after the break. It is important to know their whereabouts. Although the display of flaming boards shattering about is very effective in the technique, they nevertheless will be on fire and potentially dangerous.

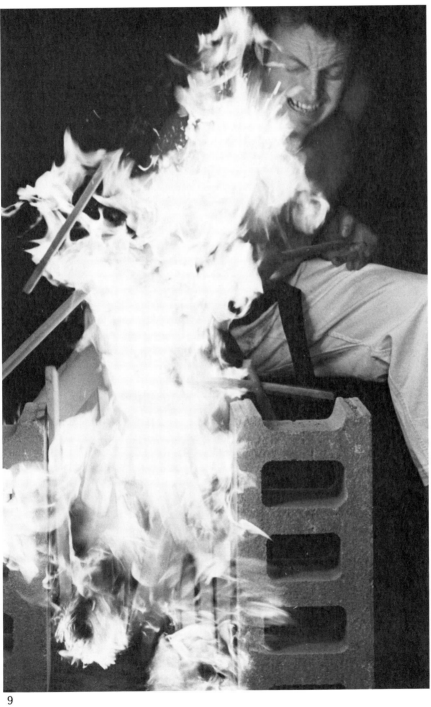

9

1

■ Swords and Daggers

Roundhouse Kick
Fig. 1

This technique demonstrates the control developed by martial arts practitioner over the movements of his body. The apple is placed on the razor-sharp edge of a samurai sword and then hit with a Roundhouse Kick to split it in half. The kick must be controlled to avoid contact with the blade. The speed of the kick must allow the leg to return to a cocked position before the apple has moved away from the blade.

Front Snap Kick
Fig. 2

The angle of the blade, illustrated in Figure 2, requires that the Front Snap Kick be aimed directly into the point. The slightest miscalculation can cause a serious puncture wound in the sole of the foot. Aside from the danger of infection, this type of injury would prevent working out because putting any pressure on the foot would be impossible.

2

3

This technique also demonstrates control over body movement. Due to its difficulty it should first be perfected with the apple hanging from a string. Once complete control is obtained, progress can be made to the use of a dull blade before advancing to razor-sharp knives or swords.

■ ■ Index